CRAFTING BREWERY CULTURE

A HUMAN RESOURCES GUIDE FOR SMALL BREWERIES

BY GARY NICHOLAS

BREWERS PUBLICATIONS

Brewers Publications®
A Division of the Brewers Association℠
PO Box 1679, Boulder, Colorado 80306-1679
BrewersAssociation.org
BrewersPublications.com

Proudly Printed in the United States of America.
10 9 8 7 6 5 4 3 2 1
ISBN-13: 978-1-938469-80-0
ISBN-10: 1-938469-80-1
EISBN: 978-1-938469-81-7

Library of Congress Control Number: 2022951686

Publisher: Kristi Switzer
Technical Editors: Joy Will, SHRM, Angela Aebersold, MHRM, SHRM-CP
Copyediting: Iain Cox
Indexing: Doug Easton
Art Direction, Cover, and Interior Design: Jason Smith
Production: Justin Petersen
Cover Letters Illustration: © GettyImages_pialhovik

To my parents, for their encouragement and
all those childhood trips to the library.

TABLE OF CONTENTS

FOREWORD

My path to a career in human resources (HR) was, in many ways, very similar to that of so many others. If you ask someone how they ended up in this profession, you'll likely hear some variation of, "I didn't start out in HR, I was a teacher/social worker/brewer . . ." (insert any seemingly unrelated job there.) I was on my way to becoming a behavior analyst when HR caught my interest.

Regardless of our initial career path, it was a desire to create an impact and help those around us that led us to this place. Whatever the individual journey looks like, formal training and HR-specific education are often lacking—an experience familiar to many individuals whose career led them to working in a craft brewery. In my case, I worked my way up to a department-of-one HR position in two separate companies. This involved learning as I went and doing a lot of independent research, before going back to school to upgrade my BS in psychology to an MBA specializing in human resources management. While the experience and on-the-job learning were invaluable, and ultimately led to my position as HR Partner for the Brewers Association, I can't emphasize enough how many times throughout my career I wished for an industry-specific resource like *Crafting Brewery Culture: A Human Resources Guide for Small Breweries*.

It seems as though the craft brewing industry was particularly slow to jump on the HR bandwagon. To an industry that, for many years, prided itself on its anti-corporate ways, what could seem more corporate than an HR department? What is generally overlooked, however, is that human resources—if done properly—is as much about advocating for the people

as it is about protecting the business. Unfortunately, when people think of HR they often think solely in terms of the latter. In the short time that I've worked in this industry, I have had numerous people share with me why they don't like or trust HR. Part of that problem stems from past interactions, oftentimes in other industries, but the other part of the problem arises from the current brewery culture. As Gary illustrates from the very beginning of this book, culture starts before a new employee is even selected for a role, and it starts within the realm of human resources.

It's no secret that the majority of craft breweries throughout the country are fairly small operations, many of which have someone managing HR while also wearing 20 (or more) other "hats" within the business as they try to get everything done and stay in compliance. I understand that position because I've been there—it's not an easy spot to be in. I want you to know that it's OK not to have all the answers. None of us have all the answers all the time, which is why we're fortunate to work in an industry whose members are known for uncompetitively sharing answers and advice with one another.

You're not alone if you're not an HR professional but happen to be managing HR in your brewery. When I joined the Brewers Association in April 2022, I was first tasked with creating a presentation at the Craft Brewers Conference® (CBC®) titled "How to Be Dedicated to HR When You Don't Have Dedicated HR." If nothing else, this should provide you some comfort knowing that it's a common enough occurrence in our industry to require a talk at the CBC. It was also the motivating factor in creating my role at the Brewers Association and the subsequent creation of the Human Resources Committee, which was built specifically to provide you with the tools needed to handle the HR part of your job, even if that is just one of many jobs you're currently holding down.

Seasoned HR professional or not, working in HR can regularly feel like a whirlwind of policies, payroll, and a mess of confidential documents. Sometimes, in all the chaos, we forget about the thing that should be top of our priority list: culture. If you're wondering where to start, or what to do next to create a strong organizational culture, then you've picked the right book. From the very first page, Gary describes the importance of the people in this industry and the business's responsibility to support and empower them. Just as the Brewers Association has dedicated itself to promoting and protecting small and independent craft breweries, HR has a responsibility to promote and protect the people who are the foundation for everything this industry has accomplished. Regardless of how large or small your brewery is, it's the people that impact productivity, product quality, and ultimately the success or failure of the business.

As you move through this book you will develop a deeper understanding of the impact that thorough training, professional development, performance management, and leadership have on your brewery's organizational culture. Gary acknowledges the history and evolution of training in the brewing industry and addresses the impact that communication and leadership have on team performance and motivation.

Despite the upfront investment required, training and feedback will ensure your team has the skills and knowledge not only to do the job, but to do the job correctly, efficiently, and safely. All these factors end up saving time and money in the long run. As HR professionals, it is our responsibility to recognize and advocate for the business components that align with the big-picture goals of our organizations and lead to successful outcomes for the people of those organizations. This often means making a business case that is solid enough to get buy-in from brewery leaders. Whether you are an HR professional by trade, or a brewery owner managing your own HR, this book provides a compelling argument for the importance of crafting a strong company culture.

Regardless of where you are in your HR career, there are always learning opportunities and room for improvement. By picking up this book, you've taken the first step in committing to continue learning and growing in your profession. *Crafting Brewery Culture* will meet you where you're at and provide practical insight and advice to help you create a workplace culture that is dedicated to protecting your team, celebrating each employee's unique contribution, and recognizing that each person plays an important role in the success of the brewery.

Holly Haslam, MBA
Human Resources Partner
Brewers Association

ACKNOWLEDGMENTS

Given that this book directly discusses mentors, I have to start by recognizing that I was incredibly fortunate with the two leaders who guided me in the early years of my career. Matt Brynildson and John Mallett had an enormous effect on how I view operations and workplace culture, and I use the lessons learned from them every single day. I am immensely grateful and hope that I pay that forward the same way.

This book would also not have happened without the people who graciously shared their time, insight, and wisdom with me for the book: Sarah Bonvallet, Dr. J Jackson-Beckham, Larry Horwitz, Katie Muggli, Elle Rhodes, Jack McCraine, Evan Meffert, Laura Mullen, and Kat Schermerhorn.

To the extent that I seem knowledgeable, it is because of the people who have influenced my thinking about brewery culture and organization over the years. There is a long list, but I'd like to particularly highlight Omar Ansari, Laura Bell, Sara Hagerty, Karl Ockert, Mary Pellettieri, Chuck Skypeck, and Carrie Yunker for providing the opportunities that led me to this point. I am also indebted to the team at SanTan Brewing for granting me time and space to complete this project.

I drew an immense amount of mental support and encouragement from friends and family throughout this process: it has meant the world to me and I will never forget it. Y'all are the best.

Finally, I am deeply indebted to Kristi Switzer, the technical editors Joy Will and Angela Aebersold, and the entire Brewers Publications team. To say that I tried their patience would be an understatement.

INTRODUCTION

As a rule, breweries are incredibly photogenic. Stainless steel vessels project an industrial cool factor combined with gravitas that is not found in most manufacturing environments. Around the corner, perhaps, a few racks of wooden barrels lend an extra degree of mystery to the space. And that's before we even get to the beer itself. The wide range of colors, enticing cap of foam, carefully curated glassware, graphic designs, and other aesthetics provide incredible imagery to help engage the public and communicate a brewery's vision. This isn't the entire picture, however. The dimension of brewing that is difficult to capture in images is the full scope of human activity that makes all this possible.

Despite all the attention understandably paid to physical equipment, employees are the most valuable assets in a brewery. How you support and empower them makes a significant difference. An effective organizational culture is as important as any process-control step or physical product test. The organizational culture that informs a workplace performs the same function as the operating systems that control modern technology. No matter how advanced the hardware or clever the applications, a haphazard operating system will quickly turn a computer, phone, or tablet into a useless brick. By the same token, well-engineered operating systems can coax impressive results from relatively basic components by making better use of precious resources, often equaling the performance of far more expensive competitors. These successful operating systems are designed to be adaptable, robust, and scalable so that they can knit together the various hardware and software components across a multitude of conditions and operational demands. The organizational culture that resides within a brewery performs the same role—the question is whether the integration is seamless or prone to errors.

At its core, a brewery is a collection of interlocking priorities and teams, where no task exists in a vacuum. Just like ripples in a pond that extend far beyond the stone's point of entry, events in the brewery can have consequences that reverberate throughout the organization. Those ripples manifest in everything affected by an action. Improperly sanitized equipment can compromise not only the beer it touches, but also lead to cross-contamination throughout the facility. Seamer issues on a canning line have an obvious direct effect on beer quality but also create additional labor and material costs, potentially even extending to distributor supply disruptions and loss of consumer confidence. While physical equipment is involved in these events, people remain at the core. Every process or procedure has a human component, either during the performance of the task or while reacting to the results. The tasks that operators accomplish, the systems they inhabit, and the decisions they make are essential to the successful long-term performance of a brewery.

MANAGING FINITE RESOURCES

The importance of making decisions is a subtle but important point. Breweries are places of action: things don't just passively happen to inanimate objects. They happen because an active decision was made by someone within the brewery. Crucially, not taking action is an active decision in its own right, and active decisions have a way of escaping the silos we think contain them.

What we prioritize will affect everything around us. Resources are always finite, no matter how much you might wish otherwise. Three core resources to monitor in a brewery setting are time, money, and attention. Whether producing 500, 5,000, or 500,000 barrels, no brewery has as much of these three resources as it would like. There are only so many hours in the day, so if you are to "create" more time, you need to develop efficiencies and find ways to increase productivity. Adding equipment and automation to increase barrels produced per labor hour can free up time. Other avenues for improving efficiency include streamlining processes to minimize waste or adding employees to spread the workload and reduce workflow bottlenecks.

Each of these avenues will cost money before benefits are realized, so making informed decisions is critical. Evaluating return on investment (ROI) is the norm when assessing new equipment and raw materials, but it's fairly common to overlook the human component, except in the context of metrics such as labor costs per barrel. While wage costs are an essential element to calculating cost of goods sold (COGS), it's important to realize that the human component isn't limited to wages. Viewing employees primarily in terms of labor costs is a reductive framing that doesn't factor in skill sets, experience, and the impact of well-designed operational procedures. While revenue can come from growth, profitability comes from preventing waste, mistakes, and errors, which is achieved via organizational culture. These preventive measures are directly tied to setting expectations, carrying out training based on those expectations, and then managing to those expectations. This concept has a direct analogue with physical assets: equipment needs preventive maintenance to function at peak levels. Investing in organizational culture is the equivalent concept for people and teams.

Unlike time and money, attention is intrinsically human: it has to be actively applied by people. Focus can be shifted from one area to another, or to nothing at all. In practice, attention indicates what we consider important at any given moment. Saying something is important isn't the same as actually following through on a consistent basis. For example, breweries can spend money on sensory evaluation programs and schedule tasting panels during the

work week, but if leadership rarely attends the panels or ignores inconvenient results, the message being sent to the staff is that those panels aren't important. Over time, that message will begin to affect how the rest of the team views the panels and, potentially, other aspects of their work.

This is where resources being finite comes into play. There may be numerous reasons behind the lack of attention paid to an area of operations. A brewery, like any organization, has multiple demands competing for its attention, especially during a growth phase. The solution to this challenge is to shift the workload from individuals juggling demands back and forth on their own to comprehensive systems that define roles and tasks that can be shared across the organization. These roles and tasks should be defined in a way that genuinely reflects the stated values and priorities of the organization.

A practical scenario may be instructive here. A common pattern among breweries when first setting up a quality assurance and quality control (QA/QC) laboratory is to place responsibility for quality issues solely on the lab. Whether consciously or not, a mindset can develop that presumes the lab technicians will be the ones to catch if something goes wrong. This is a reactive stance that is just asking for trouble. The QA/QC technician may very well catch if something is wrong, but the point is that the error has already happened. Quality isn't defined just by what we can measure after a task is complete: quality is as much about *how* we go about performing the task.

In a perfect world, quality testing would be unnecessary because every employee would do their tasks correctly every single time. Reality doesn't work that way, but that doesn't change the goal of always performing tasks correctly. An effective QA/QC program should focus on ensuring operators understand their roles and tasks, communicating specifications and corrective actions clearly, and supporting operator activity. Laboratory testing still happens, but it is there to cover the gaps, not to carry the entire responsibility for quality in the brewery. Culture is about making sure that your teams understand how responsibility and accountability are distributed within the brewery. That is equally true for safety, maintenance, sales, accounting, and hospitality/retail: the responsibility for effective performance begins with each and every member of the team.

PRIORITIES AND ACCOUNTABILITY

Priorities and accountability are what connects these efforts to manage finite resources. They are two sides of the same coin. Setting priorities is an easy concept to understand but can be difficult to execute. It is helpful to think of priorities as your organization's North Star: when in doubt, what are the guiding principles that determine your actions? In other words, what ensures you do not lose your way? Collectively, these priorities define your organizational goals and should not conflict with one another. Breweries are dynamic operations, balancing market conditions, finances, equipment, and people, all of which will change over time. Maintaining consistency—not getting lost—is a function of managing those changes, and the first step in the process is being aware of this fact.

Whatever your desired priorities may be, what happens on the brewery floor or out in the consumer-facing space is your actual organizational culture. Unfortunately, this reality doesn't always match the stated goals. What people do at the end of a long, difficult day when no one is watching is the most clear-cut test of where an organization's culture truly stands. Do they perform up to expected standards or do they take shortcuts? This is where accountability takes the stage, driving behavior toward the organization's goals and priorities. As part of this, wins should be acknowledged and celebrated, while errors need to be addressed in a timely fashion. These form a continuum and must be constantly assessed: what counts as a win one year may not look the same five years or even five weeks later. The combination of priorities and accountability will define a brewery's performance.

These priorities will naturally change over time as pressures evolve. Breweries need to be honest about their needs, resources, and capabilities. The demands on a brewery in its first few years can be very different from those experienced five or ten years later, much less twenty. Founders and early staff members often have an "all-in" mentality built around a small, highly invested team. The trouble is that running a successful brewery is a marathon, not a sprint. Opening is usually the easy part: getting the doors open is a goal with a relatively straightforward set of milestones to navigate. As chaotic and consuming as the start-up phase can be, the larger challenges arrive as staffing levels increase through organic growth and expansion and the brewery starts to experience staff turnover.

In order to establish accountability, clearly defined expectations are critical. Job functions need to be documented, with the critical aspects explained thoroughly. It is unfair to call out an employee for a mistake when the issue is essentially, "Why aren't you doing that incredibly important task I've never told you about?" The root cause of the mistake doesn't lie with the worker in this situation. Rather, it points to a lack of leadership. Repeated over time, this creates a culture of distrust and fear. Instead, organizations need to describe what success looks like for their employees by investing in thorough training.

Training is a resource-intensive activity, as we'll see in chapter 2, but the brewing process doesn't care whether you've been at the brewery for 10 years or 10 days—tasks need to be performed correctly regardless. The sooner a new employee becomes competent at their tasks, the sooner the likelihood of errors is reduced. The same holds true for the daily customer interactions that involve sales and taproom staff. Training and professional development is an ongoing process. New trends, techniques, markets, and competition will all impose their own demands on the brewery. New facilities and equipment can provide solutions, but ultimately the question comes down to whether the brewery is prepared to adapt. And that remains fundamentally a question of culture.

CULTURE CREATES RESILIENCE

resilience *noun*
re·sil·ience | \ ri-ˈzil-yən(t)s
an ability to recover from or adjust easily to misfortune or change
Merriam-Webster, s.v. "resilience (*n.*)," accessed October 8, 2021, https://www.merriam-webster.com/dictionary/resilience

The fundamentals of culture are not dependent on the size of the brewery: a 500-barrel brewery has the same basic needs as its 500,000-barrel counterpart. The specific tools used may vary according to scale, but the concepts and goals remain the same. Breweries of every size need to be capable of responding constructively to adversity and change. This capacity is the essence of resiliency.

The resilience engendered by a robust organizational culture is especially important for small organizations and those experiencing growth/expansion. Small- to medium-sized organizations tend to be grounded in relatively short time scales. It is difficult to look out for issues approaching on the horizon when you're in the trenches and dealing directly with the immediate demands of managing a business. Investing in the development of a healthy workplace culture helps smooth out the effects of unexpected challenges, while also creating space to look forward.

The resiliency of a brewery is directly connected to how it is organized. Too many demands without appropriate resources to meet them leads to burnout, while cultures that tolerate toxic behavior will and do drive people out of the industry. The traditional focus on physical equipment in our industry is not the key element here. What drives resiliency is setting achievable, realistic expectations and communicating them effectively to staff, and then managing those expectations.

WHAT THIS BOOK IS FOR

This book will lay out how to build a culture-based mindset throughout leadership and management that focuses on people as partners and employing them properly as part of resourcing the brewery. The key to building this mindset is creating an organized approach to the process of developing, managing, and maintaining the components that comprise an effective workplace culture. There is a significant body of literature on the topic of organizational culture, but this text endeavors to place lessons from that catalog into the context of a working brewery.

The first several chapters will describe how to assemble the building blocks of a resilient culture. Hiring, training, developing, and assessing employees are all examples of investments in the people who make up the core of a brewery. These topics stack onto each other and form the foundation for everything we do, from safety and quality to delivering exceptional customer service.

In the second section, the book aims to define the criteria needed to bring a culture to life and sustain it. Hiring and training are, at their core, policies. Without deliberate effort, policies become dusty three-ring binders on a shelf. Even programs that are actively in place may settle into a pattern of checking boxes and not keep up with the current needs of the brewery. Policies that were perfectly suited to the way the brewery was five years ago can provide a false sense of security about what is happening right now, much less help prepare for the future. Successful cultures are an iterative pattern, always seeking to adapt to changing environments.

DIVERSITY, EQUITY, AND INCLUSION IN THE BREWERY

The brewing industry is having a long overdue reckoning with the topic of diversity, equity, and inclusion (DEI). This book seeks to establish (1) the overall argument that DEI strengthens organizations and (2) that preparing the ground for these efforts has a positive effect on adoption and retention. This is an enormously complex issue, but acknowledging the problem is the first step. Recognizing where breweries can adjust their fundamental programs, from casting a wider net for potential job applicants to performance reviews that honestly and consistently guard against bias, is essential to building a robust organization that successfully adapts to and competes in a changing marketplace.

WHAT THIS BOOK IS NOT

To be absolutely clear, this book does not substitute for legal advice. The goal is to provide a range of essential building blocks and best practices, but the field of employment law is complex and varies dramatically between state jurisdictions. It is also not the final word on the subject of organizational cultures. Learning from experienced peers provides insights that can be adapted to your particular situation, and conference sessions (both within and outside the brewing industry) will offer more in-depth expertise.

1

HIRING: SELECTING AND BUILDING A FOUNDATION

This book is built around the principle that organizational culture drives performance. The first part of building a workplace culture is selecting the people who will be involved in your organization. Considered on a day-to-day basis, the hiring process is an aspect of brewing that easily falls out of sight and out of mind. There are moments when a hiring cycle can be anticipated, such as adding sales representatives to support increased growth or bringing in seasonal staff in advance of busy production or taproom seasons. More often, however, hiring happens on an ad hoc basis, the process starting only when staff turnover necessitates filling a position. The typical order of events is that a job posting goes up, applicants get interviewed, and a candidate is chosen.

THE TEAMBUILDING APPROACH

Picture yourself in the headquarters of a sports team. The particular sport doesn't really matter: every sports team at the professional level will go through the exercise of evaluating its season, comparing itself to the competition, and thinking critically about changes that need to happen for the team to improve and advance. Many of these decisions come down to

people, especially the players. Deciding what kinds of skills and attributes are needed for the overall team to succeed is going to be critical to deciding how to coach existing players and recruiting new ones. Now imagine the following scenario:

The season ended with a promising record, but still falling short of the playoffs. The team's owner, general manager, and coach sit around the conference room table to map out plans for next year's campaign.

Owner: *What's going to get us to the next level?*

Coach: *Well, we're going to need some new players. We were stretched thin all year.*

GM: *Plus, some of our top performers may be jumping to a rival. At least one, possibly two.*

Owner: *Okay, new players. Got it. Anything specific? Money is tight, so I want to keep payroll low wherever possible.*

Coach: *No, nothing specific. Just get us new players. As long as they're a cultural fit, we'll figure something out.*

Exactly how this process happens is a key determining factor for success. There is not a professional sporting club in the world that follows the hiring process just described. Bringing on new players during a transfer window? Absolutely. That is a staple of the sporting world. But exactly what *kind* of player needs to be brought into the squad is a carefully curated decision. Successful squads view hiring through the lens of building a team precisely because not every player brings the same attributes. Is the new team member defensively or offensively minded? Left or right-handed? Are they a recruit with immense raw talent or an experienced veteran who can set an example on the training pitch and bring stability to the squad on gameday? The needs of the team will guide what kind of players will be selected during the off-season.

UNDERSTANDING YOUR NEEDS

The same kind of carefully thought-out teambuilding approach will pay dividends when applied to breweries. You may not have an off-season per se, but hiring is a constant in any industry. The title of this chapter, "Hiring: Selecting and Building a Foundation," may seem like just an elaborate way of saying "hiring," but the full title indicates and encourages a particular mindset. The point of the exercise isn't to simply hire the first person available; it is to select a person with the right combination of skills and experience to fill a recognized need within your brewery. The selection process in the brewery starts not with hiring, but with assessing what skills are available within the existing team. How do those skills map onto the list of activities that need to be accomplished within the brewery? Where are the gaps that need to be addressed? Those gaps should drive selection decisions.

These tasks aren't limited to the brewery's production floor: they stretch across the entire breadth of the business. Whether it is a public-facing position like a taproom bartender or a non-public role like the accounting desk, every position has functions that contribute to the overall whole. Getting staff with the right combination of skills and experience to perform those functions matters to the health of the organization. Success is found through good preparatory work. Taking a casual approach to staff recruitment makes it more likely the position will need to be readvertised. Putting in the advance work to identify which skills are available in the brewery will allow you to determine the gaps that

need to be filled. Once you know what skills are needed in the brewery, you can look for that knowledge base in the candidate pool. This isn't limited to the present: you also need to think about what skills will be needed in the future. Diverse backgrounds and experiences are shown to close gaps in teams that people didn't realize they have. Different types of thinkers (with different types of life experience) approach problem-solving differently, allowing teams to evaluate situations more fully and ultimately be more innovative. Diversity, equity, and inclusion (DEI) should be a fundamental part of any organization's approach if it wants to remain resilient and retain staff.

PLAN FOR GROWTH

Future growth requirements are a critical aspect of selecting new hires. These may be technical requirements that are difficult to build from the ground up, such as bringing in specific laboratory bench skills or building a maintenance and engineering team. On the sales side, a brewery looking to expand into chain accounts will need to look for sales representatives with key account experience, as this account category operates very differently than local liquor stores, bars, and restaurants. Taprooms may look to add an events or catering manager if those avenues are seen as revenue opportunities. Any of these skills could be developed organically within the brewery, as we'll discuss in chapter 3, but the process may require more time than is realistically available to the growth plan. Either way, cataloging an inventory of skills and recognizing the gaps will pay significant dividends over the long term.

Another factor to consider is whether there is sufficient redundancy to handle staff turnover and growth. Both conditions have their own challenges. Periods of growth often start with a raw expansion phase during which there is an enormous amount of activity that is managed by throwing bodies at problems. For example, bringing a major piece of new equipment into the brewery will likely draw resources from across the company. These start with the capital expense itself, but commissioning new gear invariably requires additional staffing requirements to install, troubleshoot, and train on the equipment while also backfilling or delaying processes due to personnel being tasked to the start-up process.

These challenges aren't limited to production equipment. Launching into a new sales market successfully will involve a large amount of brewery staff and coordination; the same goes for introducing software packages for accounting or active brewery management systems. This approach suits the moment in the early days of an expansion phase, but as projects reach maturation, long-term stability is achieved by applying specific skills to problems. Achieving stability will involve many different activities; these could involve formulating standard operating procedures (SOPs) to make sure that starting conditions are correct prior to beginning production or performing market analyses on distributor depletions in

NAVIGATING A GROWTH SCENARIO

Let's consider a hypothetical brewery, Serendipity Brewing, that has successfully been running as a taproom brewery for five years. Serendipity has decided to enter the retail market with a line of canned beers. Previously, the brewery has operated an on-premises model with pre-filled crowlers (core brands) or crowlers filled to order at the bar (specialties). The leadership team has decided on a self-distribution model and will service the local metro area. The team has secured funding and production space for a multi-head filling line and is beginning the process of deciding what else the brewery needs to be successful over the long term.

Skills Map
- Wort production: No major changes are needed—a record of consistency has been established
- Fermentation and yeast management: Comfortable with this aspect, although long-term yeast management will need to be monitored as production increases
- Sales support: There is an established graphic design and social media presence within the brewery

Recognized Gaps
- Fermentation and finishing: Will need to increase focus on sanitation and dissolved oxygen pickup for shelf-life stability
- Packaging: Limited experience with can filling, seaming, and labeling, as well as packaging maintenance
- Sales: Limited retail market sales experience
- Logistics: No background in delivery or sales execution

Filling the Gaps
- Sales execution: External hires
  - Hire a sales representative with skills matched to these selected strategies
    - Direct street-level sales experience
    - Experience with forecasting and projections
    - Realistic awareness of retail shelf-life expectations
  - Hire sufficient delivery drivers and warehouse staff to manage the initial set of delivery routes
    - Decision on whether a Logistics Manager needs to be hired will depend on whether one of the founding partners takes on this role
- Quality metrics: Internal focus
  - Quantify current beer shelf stability
  - Review process controls
- Packaging and logistics: Mixed approach
  - Hire packaging experience or invest in training existing staff to take the lead role
  - Determine staffing requirements based on projections

order to build accurate sales forecasts. Note that, as a brewery grows, this pattern of increasing staffing followed by a period of investing in skills will repeat itself numerous times. With experience and familiarity, managing expansion becomes easier and less disruptive, but the basic demands of growth phases don't change. Whether you're at 2,000 barrels per year or 200,000 barrels, the core pattern remains the same: task additional people to a project while you acquire operational experience, then translate that experience into long-term stability through skills development and institutional knowledge.

THE MANY SIDES OF TURNOVER

Phases of growth require having people on hand who are committed to the brewery's ongoing plans. Nonetheless, staff turnover is a reality—this is entirely normal and can be a positive condition in many situations. Employees are people first, and each has their own goals and objectives such as further education, family situations, or employment opportunities either for themselves or a partner. Assuming that every employee will bring the same level of personal investment to the job as the founding group of employees or equity partners are expected to do is an unrealistic expectation. The goal needs to be cultivating high levels of *professional* investment, and that requires a two-way relationship.

There is a tendency to view staff leaving for industry jobs with other breweries as "training the competition." Training may not show up as a budget line item for most breweries but it is expensive nonetheless, so bearing the cost of training someone who moves on to another brewery can feel frustrating. This feeling is understandable, for sure, but it is important to look at the dynamics and what that communicates about your brewery. When employees leave to take more senior positions at other breweries, that is an upward trajectory. Building a reputation for developing team members who go on to have interesting, engaging careers elsewhere in the industry has a direct positive impact on attracting talented candidates to your own organization.

In a perfect world, career advancements would be within your brewery, but upward mobility is always a challenge in small- to medium-sized companies: there are only so many positions and promotions available. Even a lateral transfer to a brewery in another part of the country can be a positive message for recruiting. Being listed on the résumé of a strong performer reflects well on the training and work environment of your brewery, which is a competitive advantage. It also has an impact on existing staff.

POSITIVES OF TURNOVER

Sarah Bonvallet, co-founder of Dangerous Man Brewing (Minneapolis, MN), describes having people move on to other breweries as inspiring for their current staff, providing an example of how careers and business opportunities evolve. When I interviewed Sarah for this book, she explained this positive aspect of turnover: "If you really want the best for people, be willing to let them go on to new adventures authentically. The biggest compliment we can have as employers is to have team members progress in their careers and feel confident enough to start their own thing." Since Dangerous Man opened in 2013, no fewer than five of its brewers have gone on to open their own breweries. "It's fun to have former employees go on to become peers as they open their own businesses," said Sarah.

The danger is when turnover is less about upward mobility and more about expressions of frustration or more serious structural issues. Whether an employee voluntarily leaves because of frustration or has to be terminated by management because of unprofessional behavior, there is a broader situation that needs to be evaluated. These forms of turnover, while individually distinct, can point toward a troubled workplace culture that needs to be diagnosed, acknowledged, and resolved. That second point is critical: it is one thing to identify problems, but they don't get resolved if they aren't *acknowledged* as problems. This is particularly true when the issues involve behaviors and decisions inside the brewery.

JOB DESCRIPTIONS AND POSTINGS: GETTING THE WORD OUT

Whatever the reason for a new hiring cycle, setting the selection process up for success is paramount. The expense of training will be a problem for the future. The immediate concern is selecting candidates who can address the gaps in your team. This starts by determining the personal and professional characteristics you desire. Preparation is key: if you don't understand what you're looking for, it is unlikely that you'll find the right people consistently over time. The first thing that a prospective candidate will see is the job posting, so it pays to develop language that highlights your priorities.

While the posting is what the applicant sees first, a job description should guide the posting, not the other way around. Think of a job description as a new beer's recipe and specification sheet, while the posting serves as the corresponding brand sell sheet for the retail market. The goal is to define the role, establish the performance expectations, and then help potential candidates see themselves in the position.

The Job Description

First and foremost, the job description needs to communicate your values up front. Clarity and consistency are key. People respond to how they think they are being measured, so laying out what the brewery cares about is the first step. These values will depend on the brewery, but best practice examples include establishing safety, quality, and respect and equity; there may be other values that you believe should also be core priorities.

Second, the job description should accurately reflect what the expectations are for the role. The assigned tasks need to clearly lay out not just the responsibilities of the role, but also the physical requirements of working in the brewery. A well-written job description should be able to stand in as the template for a performance assessment later down the line, acting as the flip side of the same coin. The former defines the expectations, while the latter looks at how those expectations are being met.

A common phrase in job postings is "and other tasks as assigned." This line can serve an actual purpose: attempting to document every single job duty is prone to omissions and, more importantly, is blind to the changes that come with future growth. The problem is when the phrase becomes a crutch used to avoid fully thinking through what is expected, which can easily be abused. Organizations can't successfully manage to expectations if they don't put in the work to define them, putting everyone involved in a difficult position.

Another useful approach to developing job descriptions is to establish operational tiers within job categories. For example, a packaging department will have a range of skill sets and experience levels among its team members. While they are all packaging brewers, when you are trying to fill a specific operational need within the team, a generic job description will make it difficult to define the position or establish a pay rate relative to others. Establishing operational tiers such as Packaging Brewer I, Packaging Brewer II, etc. is a tool that can help to fine-tune the selection process by clearly communicating what the expectations will be. This convention also creates a clearly defined pathway for mobility within the existing team, which we will explore in greater depth in chapter 3.

The Job Posting

Once you have a job description, you can move on to creating the posting itself. The first element should be answering the question of who you are and why candidates should care about the position being described. Not everyone pays attention to the brewing industry, so don't assume that every potential candidate knows about your brewery or even the brewing industry in general. Making a case for why the position on offer is an interesting opportunity will go a long way toward attracting the candidates you want. What are your values? How are you relevant in the market? What is the pitch for someone to attach their economic fortunes to yours? This isn't markedly different than the communication techniques breweries use when trying to establish business partnerships or attract consumers. The important insight is that a job posting is a similar form of competition: the brewery is as much on display as the members of the candidate pool.

Avoiding misconceptions about the role will save time for everyone, so the next element involves defining what the job entails. Describe tasks typical of the position: candidates should be able to picture themselves doing the job. This needn't be extensive, but laying out the details is important. First, it dispels the fantasies that many people have about what being a professional brewer is like. Second, it helps to describe the position to people who have relevant skill sets but don't realize it. Being able to attract talent from industries that do not have a direct connection to brewing is a distinct competitive advantage, bringing in a broader range of knowledge bases, experiences, and viewpoints.

The next step is to present the flip side of this by describing what you are looking for in a candidate. This doesn't have to include the information from your gap analysis or precisely what you need from a teambuilding perspective, but be clear on the qualifications you expect. Make sure to avoid using jargon unless it is genuinely needed. Jargon cuts you off from talent that hasn't been exposed to brewing terminology in previous employment. During this part of the posting, there are several traps to avoid.

The Qualification Trap

The first trap involves qualifications. It is important to be honest about what you want but recognize that what you *need* is a separate issue. Writing a job posting based around the perfect candidate can end up creating a candidate profile with skills and expectations that do not correspond with the job duties, which leads to disappointment and mismatches for both the candidates and the people conducting the subsequent interviews. If you uncover the ideal candidate, fantastic, but perfection cannot be the bar for admission.

A related pitfall is focusing on titles instead of skills and traits. Job titles do not translate well within the brewing community. Being the head brewer in a full-scale production brewery encompasses a different set of skills than the day-to-day responsibilities of someone with the same title in a taproom-model brewery or brewpub setting. Could either of those people be a viable candidate for the other position? Absolutely, but information that determines that viability is in their skill set, not the title. Breweries also have a way with playing fast and loose with titles that can make it difficult to determine the applicant's actual scope of duties: "Mad Scientist," "Lead Janitor," and "Beer Wrangler" make for great business cards but aren't helpful when comparing work histories and qualifications. For that, you need actual information about the experiences and responsibilities involved in the candidate's work history.

Treating titles as keywords can also lead to candidates from outside the industry going unrecognized despite having the skills you desire. The talents and experiences that applicants bring to the table are what will add value to your team: don't close the door on industries and experiences just because the terminology used is unfamiliar. When job postings and the underlying descriptions are written well, matching applicant experience to brewery needs becomes much easier.

Finally, if you only look for people with three to five years of commercial brewing experience when posting a genuinely entry-level position, you might want to ask yourself how you got your first brewing job. Who took a chance on you, and why?

The Job Board Trap

While the first trap involves expectations, the job board trap is tied to communications: Where are these postings being advertised? Are they reaching people with the desired skills? Only shopping in one highly specialized aisle of a hardware store is going to lead to a weird and fairly limited toolbox, and the same holds true if you only advertise jobs in a limited set of forums. Mass-market job sites can be overly broad, while brewing-specific job boards can be too targeted. Packaging, maintenance, and sales skills are all incredibly transferrable, and it pays to search accordingly by advertising to a wider range of industries.

A worthwhile process is to look at where industries with operations in common with brewing are recruiting. Using maintenance as an example, beverage packaging facilities such as soda or juice bottling plants are a useful proxy. The mechanical equipment involved in beverage packaging operations has analogues across a much wider spectrum of industries. The box erector in a cereal plant operates along the same principles as a brewery's 12-pack carton erector. Even non-food operations have enormous overlap: conveyance systems, sensor packages, and programmable logic controllers are present in virtually every packaging application.

The willingness to look beyond the familiar continues to pay dividends when applied to industries without clear brewery-related connections. Think about where pools of talent may exist that have the skills you're looking for and make the effort to reach out to them. In addition to industries with directly related skills and equipment, reach out to local community colleges and trade schools. These organizations typically will have job boards and are excellent reservoirs of talent, with people who are actively looking to transition careers as well as those just entering the job market for the first time. Another group whose relevant skills are frequently overlooked or misunderstood are those with military service.

THE DIVERSITY CONJECTURE

In the preface to his book, *The Difference*, Scott E. Page (2007, xiv) describes diversity as "differences in how people see, categorize, understand, and go about improving the world." Page posits a straightforward idea: diversity leads to better outcomes (2007, 4). The book goes on to explore how these differences lead to improved problem-solving. The same observation is echoed across a wide range of management literature. Making the effort to recruit a range of voices and experiences strengthens an organization.

RECRUITING OUTSIDE THE BOX

Once a brewery decides that it needs to expand its recruitment pool, an important factor is reducing the notion that direct experience in the field is needed. Many owners and managers make this a "requirement," but then don't apply it to people they happen to know, directly or peripherally, who don't have any experience in the industry. Whether they realize it or not, they are gatekeeping otherwise qualified candidates.

—Elle Rhodes
Director of Sales, Du Nord Spirits

BEST PRACTICES FOR INTERNAL POSTINGS

- **Advance notice:** Posting the position internally a week prior to the public announcement gives employees time to prepare and be on a level playing field with outside candidates actively seeking interviews.
- **Offer informational interviews:** Provide enough information for employees to decide whether to formally enter the process. This saves time for everyone and can be done via groups or individually.
- **Fast-track internal candidates to the first phase of face-to-face interviews:** Since they're currently working for you, they've already provided the kind of information that you would glean from a phone interview. The question is whether their skills translate to the new position, so extend the professional courtesy of going through the job description in person and providing them the opportunity to make their case for advancement.
- **Be honest about your process and decisions:** Operate in good faith with your employees and talk them through how you make selections.

Internal postings are another valuable resource. Don't sleep on the previous experience and schooling hidden amidst your current employees. Drawing upon the talents throughout your staff can create a pipeline for production, sales, graphics support, or administrative needs within the brewery. People enter the industry with a wide variety of skills from previous experiences, and they may be ready to transition again into a new role within the brewery if given the opportunity. The same holds true for people who start in one position and then find an unexpected aptitude and interest for other tasks. You already have a window into their work ethic and job performance. They may not be the right candidate, but the key here is to at least offer them the opportunity to compete for upcoming roles.

The Compensation Trap
The final trap when creating a job posting involves compensation. Discovering the pay scale for a position shouldn't be an obstacle course for the candidate. If you know what wage scale you're offering, say what it is. Several states actually require disclosure, either in the job posting itself or upon request by an applicant. There is a fundamental lack of equity when employers expect applicants to honestly state their current wages but then play their own cards close to their chest. There is nothing wrong with pay rates being dependent on experience, but stating the range you've budgeted for isn't a burden. The operational tiers described earlier come into play here and can help define expectations regarding responsibilities and experience.

Candidates with experience can and should argue their case. If the job description is well-defined, together you will be able to find the point where value added matches the compensation being offered. There is a temptation to wait until you have finalists before revealing pay rates. This wastes time if the favored candidates are outside your budget and promptly reject the offer at the end of the process when they hear the wage. Best case, you've lost time during the process. Worst case, you have to re-open the search and hope that other candidates have not moved on. Repeatedly advertising for the exact same position sends a signal of its own and it isn't a positive one. You also may miss out on skilled candidates who might have applied if provided with more information from the outset, due to them expecting to be priced out on either the high or low side.

RÉSUMÉ REVIEWS AND INTERACTIVE INTERVIEWS: GATHERING INFORMATION

Once a job has been posted, the transition to evaluating candidates can begin. During the initial application and résumé sweep, keywords remain a useful tool provided they are broad enough to identify the target skills across a variety of industries. Remember, the goal is to search for the skills and qualities you want to add to the team.

Résumé Review

When evaluating résumés, make sure that you're reading them alongside the job description. Most résumés submitted will be fairly generalized and not tailored to the position you posted, which can be frustrating, but try to keep an open mind. For the first pass through a stack of résumés, if the work experience described connects with the job description, set it in the review pile. The goal isn't to make an immediate decision, it is to uncover potential to assess later.

Cover letters serve an important purpose, but that purpose isn't to create an artificial barrier at the start of the selection process. Fundamentally, cover letters exist to fill in gaps and explain aspects of work history that may not be apparent from a straight reading of the résumé. Major career transitions and gaps in employment are obvious examples, and cover letters can also provide a platform for candidates to dive into an area and provide greater context about how that experience relates to the job posted. In short, cover letters are tools for the job applicants, not the employer. Requiring

a cover letter without a clear purpose is a pointless burden for both the applicant and the reviewer.

When working with application platforms, consider that duplication can be deadly. Requiring people to submit a résumé and then re-type all that information into an application form is just as likely to discourage a high-potential candidate as anyone else. Paper job applications have been around forever, with the unfortunate result that, as more and more administrative tasks go digital, many cloud-based applicant tracking systems have carried some of the same weaknesses into the digital realm. Application forms can also promote inequity through a variety of means. For example, requiring applicants to disclose past pay rates—a common feature—comes across as invasive (because it is), especially for job postings that often don't include the pay scale being offered. The problem becomes worse when the system isn't actually used for every posting, so certain applicants can just ignore requirements imposed on others.

Application platforms can offer a common framework for all applicants, and applicant tracking systems offer very real advantages. As the employer, your challenge is to promote the positive aspects and discard the portions that only exacerbate inequity and exclusion.

Interviewing

Once you've identified applicants with potential, you need to develop interview questions and formats that will identify candidates with the specific qualities you're searching for. If the questions aren't targeted, drawing out the necessary information to make an informed decision will be a function of luck. Questions should be designed so that they are tied to the role itself and the expectation of the job. Look for traits and demonstrated experience, not jargon. Just because someone has brewery experience doesn't mean they're actually good at their craft or suited to the operations at your facility. Questions should tease out how candidates approach realistic situations. Time is valuable, so each question should have a purpose. Equally important, the people conducting the interview need to understand the purpose of the questions and what criteria they're supposed to be looking for in the answers.

For critical aspects, asking complementary questions helps get past rote, practiced answers, revealing how a candidate really thinks about the topic. Personality testing systems such as Myers–Briggs, Enneagram, Big Five, and emotional intelligence scoring all use this technique, asking variations of the same basic questions in a variety of phrasings and scenarios to control for inconsistency and get around the dreaded aspirational-but-not-honest answer.[1] While personality testing systems themselves have debatable utility, the practice of asking related

DO APPLICATION PLATFORMS HAVE THEIR PLACE?

Many companies use an applicant tracking system (ATS) to help manage their applicant pools. There is a significant upside: having all the applicants for a specific job compiled in one place reduces the likelihood of a candidate slipping between the cracks. In addition, an ATS can simplify communication between the brewery and candidates, particularly the ones who don't move forward in the application process. Rejection is never fun, but knowing that they're not moving forward in the process allows former candidates to move on.

Applicant tracking systems are also a way to track and identify patterns of racism and other forms of discrimination. In the old days, you could literally feel the difference between expensive résumé paper and Kinko's-grade paper. That created an access and bias issue, and this hasn't gone away. Electronic copies have resolved that to a degree.

Requiring a stand-alone application is a different thing, and it is important to distinguish between the two. Applications used to be paper forms that could be filled out by prospective employees in lieu of a written résumé. They're particularly well-suited to positions and industries that have common skills sets across individual employers, such as the hospitality sector. They've now been implemented in digital form, often as part of an ATS. Whether paper or electronic, a truism is that the longer the form, the less likely it is that prospective staff will actually complete it. This is especially true if the form arbitrarily requires applicants to list a long series of previous employers and expects names and contact information for former supervisors. It sounds reasonable, but time is a resource and lengthy forms become a barrier to entry.

Duplication is another flaw. If the job posting calls for a résumé and then still forces an applicant to re-type most of that information into an application form in order to get into the system, it is incredibly frustrating and unnecessary. A best practice is to allow applicants to submit in either format. Résumés can be scanned and attached as a pdf to an ATS entry.

A well-managed application program can help promote equity and inclusion by creating a common format for all applicants, but the key phrase here is "well-managed." There is a difference between having internet access and having regular internet access. If the ATS platform isn't accessible through mobile devices, it can artificially eliminate qualified candidates who are transitioning between living arrangements or don't have the financial reserves to readily replace equipment. You should make it a requirement of your ATS that the online application process can be handled equally well on a personal computer, handheld device, or a library terminal. Even then, be mindful of applicants' circumstances and don't assume immediate responses are always feasible.

If you are considering an ATS, the golden rule is that the application platform needs to simplify the process, not needlessly complicate it.

---

[1]   For example, as much as you want your Dungeons & Dragons character to be Neutral Good, honestly answering any of the various alignment questionnaires inevitably leads to a result of Lawful Neutral.

questions to draw out actual information instead of rehearsed soundbites has significant value. For example, several of the example questions in the sidebar on page 16 below are deliberately complementary. Answers to the question about work environments can be compared to those about making time-sensitive decisions. Do they mesh or contradict each other? Follow-up questions can tease out additional information to resolve minor inconsistencies and more serious concerns.

Avoiding closed-loop questions is an important factor when setting up a successful interview process.

A closed-loop question is defined by having a limited, if not binary, set of responses. For example, "Do you consider quality to be important for breweries?" isn't likely to yield much useful information unless someone actually disqualifies themselves by saying "No, it isn't important." The format of the question doesn't require elaboration or encourage the candidate to open up about how they would perform in the role. This format makes it easy to game the system and say what an interviewer wants to hear. A better form of the question would be, "How do you define a quality-driven organization?

EXAMPLES OF INTERVIEW QUESTIONS

Please take me through your work history and provide a brief overview of what you learned from each position and how that led you to where you are today.

Purpose: Résumés can only say so much. Get a sense of the candidate's experience and let them describe their career arc in their own words. Follow up on career transitions and assess their adaptability. Do they share the brewery's core values or are there red flags?

What is it about this role that motivated you to apply?

Purpose: Determine what it is about this role the candidate is passionate about and what interests them about the brewery. Look for mismatches between their expectations and the reality of the role.

Describe to me the type of work environment you thrive in, and why?

Purpose: What is the candidate looking for in a job? Ask follow-ups to get a sense of whether they understand the work environment and can adapt to the brewery's core values and priorities.

Tell me about a time when you had to make a time-sensitive decision based on limited information. What was the situation and how did you influence the process?

Purpose: Get to know the candidate's communication style and how they deal with their peers.

Based on what this role entails, can you tell me how you would add value right away?

Purpose: Confirm whether the candidate understands the role and can identify key attributes needed to be successful.

What questions do you have for me, either about the role or the company overall?

Purpose: Is the candidate an active participant in the interview or just going through the motions? Are they making an informed decision on their end?

What does that look like to you?" The goal is to unveil what you need to know about how a candidate will perform and provide enough information to compare applicants accurately and fairly.

Open-loop, or open-ended, questions are vastly more useful by virtue of putting the applicants in a position to describe their thought process and approaches to handling various situations. These situations should be tied to the job description itself and company values. Interviewers should guard against falling into conversations rather than performance-related questions. There is nothing wrong with a conversational tone in an interview; it is usually preferable to a more interrogative format. The problem is when the conversational tone and approach supersedes the purpose of the interview. It is incredibly easy to chat about common interests such as mutual contacts, beer trends, or music and risk losing the thread of the interview. Stay on target. The goal of the exercise is to identify the next member of your team, not trade stories.

A related issue arises when interviewers use different sets of questions across the candidate pool. Interview questions should have purpose and intent directed at learning how people would operate in your brewery. When you do not ask broadly similar questions to different candidates, you lose the ability to compare apples to apples when reviewing applicant answers later during the evaluation phase. Asking the same questions of all the candidates to consistently evaluate candidates is a DEI best practice.

Again, interviews don't need to be strictly formal or regimented: conversational approaches work. The point is that the interview should cover each of the relevant topics, and it is easy for material to be overlooked if the conversation starts to wander. If a candidate has already addressed a point in an earlier answer, an interviewer may always ask, "You answered this in the previous question, but do you have anything to add?" It is okay to tailor questions to each candidate's work history, but the main questions should be the same.

Questions aren't the only techniques for finding information relevant to the skill sets and actual job requirements. In fact, providing a practical exercise component has several advantages when interviewing candidates. First, they can be directly tailored to the position and provide a platform for candidates to demonstrate their knowledge. Second, it helps to control for differences between people who happen to interview well and those who aren't as comfortable in the format but can absolutely do the job.

EVALUATION AND SELECTION: COMPARE AND CONTRAST

An essential part of the evaluation process is making sure that the people looking through the résumés and conducting interviews understand what you are looking for. This should have been determined when writing the job description, but writing a job description isn't always the same thing as communicating the information to the people who will do the initial résumé sweep. Most breweries do not have dedicated HR personnel, especially among small- to medium-sized operations. In small breweries, the individuals establishing the selection criteria and reviewing applicants may be one and the same. As staff size increases, however, gaps can develop, so it's important to ensure that the execution follows your intent.

When conducting interviews or reviewing notes afterward, it is important to guard against interviewer biases. These can be unconscious or conscious and can take a variety of forms. Employment law directly references certain biases, such as those relating to race or gender, but personal preferences can also influence the outcome. A useful tool to maintain a fact-based approach is the STAR technique.[2] This is a behavioral interview technique that specifically seeks out concrete, metrics-based situations the candidate has faced and separates them from hypothetical scenarios. It is still vulnerable to interviewer bias, but the format provides a reference point to check against.

Note that several of the sample interview questions listed above (see "Examples of Interview Questions" on p. 16) are specifically constructed to elicit concrete responses. The idea is to get a better sense of how a candidate has performed in the past and would likely act in the future, rather than wax on about an idealized version of themselves. There will always be a measure of casting oneself in the best light possible: the interview process is naturally an exercise in self-promotion, after all. When the terms of the conversation are largely hypothetical, it becomes easy for candidates to play to the crowd and respond to questions with answers that

---

2   "STAR Method," Behavioral Interviewing, Development Dimensions International, Inc., accessed October 30, 2022,
      https://www.ddiworld.com/solutions/behavioral-interviewing/star-method.

they think you want to hear. Basing the interview on specifics helps to cut through that tendency.

Having a clear, repeatable framework for evaluating job applicants is the first step toward establishing a level playing field and identifying those candidates who could be successful within your organization. There are other hurdles that you need to address,

however, that have more to do with organizational biases than the candidates themselves.

The "Culture Fit" Fallacy

Asking whether a candidate is a cultural fit for a company is a common trope within organizations, particularly during the hiring phase. It's an attractive

OPTIONS FOR DEMONSTRATION-BASED INTERVIEW TECHNIQUES

Sales
- **Task:** Provide a sell sheet in advance and ask the candidate to simulate pitching an account on that beer during the interview.
- **Metric:** How do they organize their pitch and what do they prioritize?

Maintenance
- **Task:** Ask the candidate to lock out an unfamiliar piece of equipment with multiple energy sources.
- **Metric:** Do they systematically and thoroughly de-energize the machinery?

Tour guides
- **Task:** Ask the candidate to prepare a five-minute presentation on any topic they are passionate about and deliver it at the interview.
- **Metric:** How engaging are they when talking about an issue they already know and care about?

Training staff
- **Task:** Ask the candidate to be prepared to teach tying a knot of their choice to the interview team.
- **Metric:** How do they approach a lesson plan? Do they try to accommodate different learning styles?

DIRECT WORK EXPERIENCE: INTERNSHIPS, STAGES, AND SHORT-TERM CONTRACTS

Another way to gain insight about a potential team member is through short-term work experience within the organization. Opportunities such as paid internships offer a way to get to know individuals in the relevant work environment over time without the pressures of an interview. Within the culinary world, *stages* are a way to provide a chef with a temporary residence at another restaurant to share techniques between kitchens, but they are also used to evaluate an aspiring cook's practical skills over several shifts before committing to a formal job offer. The same technique could be used within the brewery setting. Seasonal work contracts offer another path for both temporary workers and employers to assess one another and provide a known talent pool for when long-term positions open up.

Regardless of the exact format, there is a legal obligation for these trial experiences to be paid and they must adhere to safety training requirements. In addition to the legal and regulatory aspects, there is an ethical component: not paying people for their labor narrows your candidate pool to those who don't need those wages to cover their living expenses, eliminating otherwise qualified candidates from even applying.

concept. This entire book is premised on the notion that a healthy organizational culture is central to successful operations. It makes sense that you would want to hire people who will fit into that healthy culture and filtering applicants through this metric would seem to be an obvious step. The problem is that looking for a cultural fit can lead to dark and dangerous paths. At best, the approach makes it easy to focus on a candidate's interests and hobbies instead of their relevant skills. At worst, it becomes a way to exclude people from the industry, either consciously or not.

This starts with the tendency to hire people who are similar to you (Jackson-Beckham 2022). That's an understandable tendency, but it misses the whole point of a selection system, which is shoring up weaknesses and adding strengths to your teams. Looking for a "culture fit" involves deciding whether a candidate will fit in with the existing team through the lens of what you're comfortable and familiar with. Without stringent checks and balances in place, this easily becomes a subjective judgment that masquerades as an objective assessment.

FOCUS ON SKILLS, NOT FAMILIARITY

Passion counts for a lot, but you need to be intentional when you're building a team. Look for the skills you need, not titles or relationships. It's also important to recognize that the skills you need can come from a variety of industries. Think through

USING THE STAR METHOD TO DRAW OUT INFORMATION

Not every qualified candidate will be comfortable or skilled with describing their experience and talents in an interview context. One way to bridge that gap is to provide a structure that helps them navigate open-ended questions and better reveal their skill sets. A common technique is the STAR method. The STAR acronym stands for Situation, Task, Action, Result:

Situation: Look for situations that resulted in an outcome.

Task(s): Define the actual tasks involved.

Action(s):
- Look for specific actions that the candidate performed or examples of behaviors that indicate how they approach situations.
- Listen for the use of "I" versus "we" and the context in which they are used. This can be tricky, but it creates ample opportunities for follow-up questions.
  - The use of "I" can describe how the individual performed or be a sign that they are taking credit for the work of others.
  - The use of "we" may indicate a team-based leadership mentality or point to someone who floated through a project on the work of others.

Results:
- What were the outcomes?
- Does the candidate use specific measurable examples?

The STAR method is particularly well-suited to structuring follow-up questions. There are two notable advantages to this approach. First, it helps to cut through meandering or irrelevant responses. More importantly, however, the technique levels the playing field for viable candidates who haven't had extensive interview experience or training. By helping them focus answers toward specific actions and outcomes, you're better able to identify and compare qualified candidates.

what skills an applicant would have gained from prior employment.

When I interviewed Elle Rhodes, Director of Sales at Du Nord Spirits, for this book, she listed the multiple industries in which she had worked before joining a brewery as a sales representative, which included investment and interior design and running her own inventory management firm. When joining the brewery, Rhodes could bring to bear the following skills:

Interior design

- **Aesthetics:** experience working with color and shape relationships directly related to working on beer brand redesigns and thinking through how they would appear next to other brands in the market
- **Customer management:** experience navigating negotiations with potentially difficult clients and high-value but personality-driven relationships

Inventory management

- Fluency in spreadsheets, forecasting, and product flow
- From managing her own firm, Rhodes was deeply aware of the financial aspect of managing a business, both her own and those of clients.

If the owners had focused solely on industry relationships, they would have missed how Rhodes' set of skills would translate into the beer world.

Cultures are additive structures, not predetermined designs. A former US ambassador to the UK, Matthew Barzun, draws an analogy through the history of the Great Seal of the United States (Barzun 2021, 17–18). If you're unfamiliar with the design, look at the back of a US one-dollar bill, where both sides of the seal are represented. The eyes are naturally drawn to the pyramid on the left side. What Barzun points out is that this is not the front of the seal: it's the reverse side. Nor is it where the phrase *e pluribus unum* appears. Placing the Latin motto for "out of many, one" next to the pyramid would imply that, in order to be a member of the organization, you have to fit into a rigid hierarchical structure. Instead, the phrase, which is written on the front of the seal, is set underneath a constellation of thirteen stars, referred to as a "radiant constellation" in the original design. Each star exists on its own but is part of a greater whole. The metaphor for a young democracy was that

adding new states wouldn't displace the existing ones: they would simply expand the constellation. The recipe for growth embedded in this idea is that the strength of an organization is based on its variety.

The same metaphor holds when building teams inside the brewery. Dr. J Jackson-Beckham, founder and principal of Crafted For All, LLC and Equity and Inclusion Partner for the Brewers Association, links this idea directly to team building: hire for *cultural growth*, rather than cultural fit. Other organizations refer to this concept as looking for "cultural additions." This approach helps future-proof an organization as it grows, building out a robust, diverse array of skills and viewpoints. Predetermined structures are static, whereas constellations are dynamic. This dynamism is what makes an organizational culture healthy and allows for growth. Bringing a variety of skills, experiences, and viewpoints to the table creates the flexibility essential to problem-solving, recognizing opportunities, and addressing flaws.

Redefining "Fit"

There is a tension that becomes apparent at this point. The early argument in this chapter was that establishing and communicating a clear set of values is essential to a selection process, but now using culture fit as a selection tool is discouraged. Given that, how are you supposed to identify people who share those values? What should you be looking for? The idea of "fit" is real, but how you assess it matters. The resolution to this tension has two components: aptitude and attitude.

Aptitude can best be defined as "How do the applicant's skills and experience map onto the needs from our gap analysis?" This is a largely objective measure. They either have applicable skills or they don't, and a set of résumés can be scored side-by-side on how well they match up to the gap analysis and the job description itself. Note that aptitude allows for a measure of flexibility when comparing résumés. A candidate who performs their own motorcycle maintenance may be a better fit for an assistant brewer position in a small brewery than the candidate who has five years of experience in a fully automated brewhouse with dedicated support departments. This is where understanding your specific needs comes into play. You may want the process experience of the production brewer because of your own growth plans, or you may want the hands-on troubleshooting experience of a practiced motorcycle mechanic. Either way, the person you hire will have knowledge gaps that you will have to fill so that they can successfully operate in your facility, which involves training. This puts the entire candidate pool on equal footing when assessing the skills any one candidate would add to the brewery.

Attitude approaches the concept of fit from a different angle by asking questions such as "How does the applicant approach challenges?" Do they first look for solutions or call for help? Do they have an awareness of the overall picture or do they fixate on details? How do they work through difficult situations? This is an inherently more subjective assessment, but the questions involved are directly targeted at job-related performance and are forward-looking, which helps to evaluate growth potential.

When evaluating aptitude and attitude, it is important to meet candidates where they're at and put in the work to understand what they are telling you. A recent college or high-school graduate applying for an entry-level position isn't likely to have an extensive work history to draw from, so provide them with the space to apply your questions to the experiences they do have. The same holds true when looking at candidates from unfamiliar industries. There is a difference between a candidate not answering a question well because of lack of experience and one not answering well because she was an E-5 in a military aviation maintenance unit and isn't sure how to fully explain what that entails in a civilian setting. People with gaps in their work history or career transitions have similar challenges. Likewise, a résumé with a pattern of bouncing from job to job every two years might indicate a red flag about the candidate's professional behavior, but there may be other reasons that explain the pattern. If the overall package is interesting, ask the applicant to fill in the gaps. Dismissing such candidates early in the process because they don't seem like a "good fit" unnecessarily limits your talent pool. Combining a deep understanding of what you are looking for with a measure of imagination and patience can pay significant dividends, both immediately and over the long term as the brewery grows.

Speaking of the long term, generational differences also appear during interviews and evaluations. (Table 1.1 shows commonly accepted ranges of birth years

for Gen X, Millennials, and Gen Z.) The idea that "no one wants to work anymore" isn't new: newspaper clippings with variations on this theme have reliably appeared in every decade dating back to the eighteenth century. Nor is it accurate: the disconnect stems from how different generations approach work and the experiences they see in the world around them. A person's view of the workplace is deeply influenced by the societal realities they experienced growing up.

Millennials are on track to be the first generation in the modern era to earn less than their parents.[3] The reasons are complex and outside the scope of this book, but the financial collapse of 2008 and its aftereffects occurred right as many Millennials were entering the job market, and while interest rates dropped to historical lows, student debt rose to historic highs. Despite that, surveys indicate that the reputation of job-hopping Millennials isn't true: they remain with employers at roughly the same rate as Gen X workers. What is different is that Millennials are more likely to embrace diversity and inclusion and have a tendency to prioritize work that emphasizes values and purpose (Sinek 2014, 291). Directly communicating a brewery's values and making sure that you adhere to them is important.

Gen Z occupies a unique space. They grew up with the internet and social media, not knowing a world without them: the first wave of Gen Z was only 10 years old when the iPhone was introduced. There is a notion that this has led to them job-hopping because they get distracted. What surveys show, however, is that Gen Z is motivated by flexibility and professional advancement. Building a robust professional development pathway is a significant recruitment and retention advantage (see chap. 3).

Table 1.1 **Defining generational ranges**

Generation	Birth Years for Selected Generations	
	Pew Research Center	**JCHS[a]**
Gen X	1965–1980	1965–1984
Millennial	1981–1996	1985–2004
Gen Z	1997–	2005–

Sources: Ranges from Dimock (2019); Masnick (2017).
Notes: The Pew Research Center uses 15-year ranges to define generations, but other groups prefer 20-year bands.
[a] Joint Center for Housing Studies, Harvard University

---

3   Kristen Bialik, Richard Fry, "Millennial life: How young adulthood today compares with prior generations," Pew Research Center, February 14, 2019, https://www.pewresearch.org/social-trends/?p=25828.

Selection—and Rejection—of Applicants

Talking about "fit" is cool and all, but how do you make a decision? It's a fair question: theory isn't practice, and the point of the exercise is to create a hiring process that identifies the brewery's personnel needs and selects candidates who will be successful in those tasks. The immediate answer isn't picking the person you want a beer with. Resilient organizations are additive cultures, not pre-defined social groups, so personal connections aren't as predictive as they might appear. It's tempting to look for a formula, but people aren't math and hiring isn't an equation. When you start to evaluate your candidates, you want to be able compare apples to apples: this is literally why the format you use to ask questions matters. This starts at the application/résumé level and extends through the interviews.

There are multiple ways to approach the task of selecting prospective candidates, but we'll focus on four main components:

- Give applications multiple readings
- Use fact-based criteria and be forward-looking to allow for growth
- Categorize and rank prospective candidates
- Handle rejections tactfully

Give Applications Multiple Readings

First, treat the résumé and interview phase as an iterative process. Each pass through a stack of résumés will narrow the list of candidates by applying an ever more rigorous set of criteria until you've identified the applicants you want to interview. Trying to make a final decision from a single read of an application is akin to tasting beers in a competition one at a time and deciding on a best in show without actually evaluating the rest of the field. Either you'll pick the first beer you find appealing, or you'll fall victim to the last sample bias. That's a terrible way to judge beers and an even worse way to pick someone for a job. Instead, each pass-through of prospective candidates should have criteria that will determine who moves on to the next round. From there, you'll fine-tune your criteria with each successive pass. The same will hold true with the interview phase, using complementary questions to dig into the details with each candidate.

Use Fact-Based Criteria and Be Forward-Looking to Allow for Growth

The criteria you use during successive passes through applications and candidate questions will define your second component. Right from the outset, you can scan a résumé or interview a candidate and get a sense of their ability to perform the tasks as written

INTERVIEW PHASES AND METRICS

Interview – Initial

- Be brief—phone interviews are fine.
  - The point is to keep it simple and in the 15 to 30-minute range.
  - This phase can also function as the verbal equivalent of a cover letter for applicants, giving them an opportunity to volunteer more information. If there are further questions, ask them in the next round.
- Metrics
  - Look for core skills from the job description.

Interview – Second round

- A second-round interview is all you will need for most positions.
  - Dig into details from the resumé, work history, and the position itself.
  - Demonstration-based questions are appropriate at this stage.

Interview – Third round

- Every candidate invited to the third-round interview should be capable of performing the position as written.
- Metrics
  - Look for what they bring to the table compared to other candidates
  - Ask how the candidate adds value to your
    - current operations,
    - future operations, and
    - existing team.

in the job description. Remember to remain open to non-obvious or non-traditional career paths: there are a wide variety of experiences that can lead to the mixture of aptitude and attitude that you want to add to your existing teams. Be metric-based: "He seems cool" isn't a metric. It's also important to remember that job requirements are not the same as your ideal set of attributes. Requirements describe what you *need*, while ideals describe what you *want*. Rejecting competence in hopes of finding perfection limits your options and doesn't do justice to the overall field. It's useful to ask, "Would I have been hired if I had been held to the same expectations when I was at that point in my career?" If the answer is "No," reflect on what the difference is and whether it serves a useful purpose today.

You should also hold yourself to the core values you identified when developing the job description. A seemingly ideal candidate who doesn't share these core values should be a no-go. Don't get sucked in and overlook problems: core values matter, otherwise they aren't core values.

From there, it is useful to look at growth opportunities: Of the candidates available, who offers the most potential over the long-term? There are several ways to assess this, including adaptability and flexibility in the current system, as well as skills that you may not need right away but could pay dividends in the future as you grow both in volume and in complexity. The most important example of the latter is leadership potential. A proven track record of leadership experience is exceptionally valuable.

Categorize and Rank Prospective Candidates
The third component in this process is having a way to fairly sort and compare candidates. Again, there isn't one right technique available, but one option is a categorization technique called *stack ranking*. This term has recently caught on in the tech industry, but the basic idea has long been used by search firms and talent acquisition staff in a variety of arenas. One word of caution: this concept has been abused, most notably in performance evaluations, so it is critical to be careful how it is applied.

The basic idea is to sort candidates into a series of "stacks" or tiers. For sake of ease, using three groups offers enough flexibility without introducing unwieldy complexity:

- Group A: Small group, clearly have the desired skills and bring more to the table
- Group B: Most of the puzzle pieces are apparent, just need to dig deeper to complete the picture. Diamonds in the rough lurk here.
- Group C: Time is valuable. Move on.

One advantage of this technique is the ranking structure to categorize applicants can be reset and reused at each stage of the recruitment process. An applicant sorted into group A based on their résumé may drop to groups B or C after the interview phase. Likewise, a group B applicant on the basis of their résumé may rise into group A after an interview: people aren't two-dimensional pieces of paper. Another advantage is that it helps to create and enforce some time management into the process. If there are enough candidates in group A, focus your attention on them. If the field is more limited, draw one or more of the most interesting group B candidates into the process so that you can actually make a comparison. This doesn't mean that you should interview someone you have no intent of hiring—that is a waste of time for everyone involved. The point is to have sufficient variety within the interview pool that there are actual contrasts between candidates to help make the most educated and informed choice possible.

Another useful attribute to building out candidate tiers is that it allows you to document your selection process and genuinely evaluate your recruiting process. Being faced with limited options for viable candidates is frequently a sign that your outreach efforts are equally limited, either from job postings that aren't crafted in a way that attracts interesting candidates or because the postings aren't reaching those candidates. Even professional brewing job boards can be limited in scope: looking at who is making it to your A and B groups can tell you a lot about the limitations of your recruiting process. In keeping with the corporate adage that you can't manage what you don't measure, tracking your selection and recruitment pool helps to inform the process and uncover biases that may have slipped in by helping you show your math.

For all the positives associated with stack ranking, there are cons. For one thing, selection and hiring isn't a neat equation. People aren't commodities, and there won't be neat boundaries between the tiers you build out. Navigating that gray area between candidate groupings can pose challenges, particularly because ranking candidates into groups can amplify biases if you aren't careful about focusing on aptitude and attitude instead of the false comfort of "culture fit." It can also be difficult to quantify the future upsides a candidate may offer, but this is a challenge for any ranking system. In practical terms, the reality is that immediate needs are the priority when you are filling a hole within the existing structure versus preparing for the future. The key thing to keep in mind is that stack ranking is a first pass technique for categorization, not a determinative step.

Handle Rejections Tactfully

The fourth and final component you should consider is how to deal with the fact that you're not going to hire everyone who applied for a position. Even when you have two finalists you would gladly welcome into your brewery, one of them is going to get the short phone call unless you have the budget to hire both. How you let candidates know that they weren't selected says a lot about your organization and can absolutely affect how your future job postings are perceived by prospective candidates and the wider professional community. No one likes to be ghosted or feel rejected. Courtesy goes a long way toward preventing the disappointment in not being selected from feeling like a personal rejection.

The fact is that past candidates may be candidates again in the future when circumstances make them an ideal choice for the position. Memories of disrespect can easily lead to them passing on the opportunity, and those rejected candidates generally also have friends and colleagues—impressions matter. On a more personal note, career paths are weird: you may end up applying for a job with someone you rejected. Or one of their friends. Again, impressions matter. The phrase "courtesy is free" comes to mind, but the reality is that it does take time. Particularly during the initial phase of reviewing résumés, it may not feel like this is time well spent, but I would argue the opposite. In addition to affecting future candidate pools, there is a community reputation component: how people feel about a brewery has as much impact on its success as the beer itself. Negatives linger far longer in the public consciousness than positive stories.

Managing this process using an applicant tracking system allows you to automate the early rounds. Third-party job boards like Indeed or Monster are a challenge

COMMON PITFALLS WHEN SELECTING NEW HIRES

- During the preparation phase
  - Not understanding or communicating what you're looking for in a candidate
  - Not presenting a clear picture of what it's like to work for the brewery: you expect an applicant to be honest about how they approach their work, so make sure you're as honest about the work environment
- During the interview phase:
  - Not asking questions that are relevant to the skill sets and actual job requirements
  - Falling into conversations rather than useful questions
  - Asking closed-loop questions
  - Asking different questions to different candidates: you lose the ability to compare apples to apples
- During the selection phase
  - The tendency to hire people who are like you
  - Focusing on immediate needs instead of potential for growth or future needs

they also have similar tools available. Even if you are using automated tools, courtesy still matters. Write the rejection notice you would want to receive if you were an applicant. You don't need to re-invent the wheel: a well-written form letter is better than silence. Basic email tools like blind carbon copy (bcc) are your friend.

The further through the process an applicant goes, the more important a genuine touch is. Remember, the applicants you interview are investing as much time as you are, often more so if they prepared for the interview. It can be difficult, especially if you are conflict-averse, but taking the time to deliver the news politely and respectfully to unsuccessful candidates is a worthwhile exercise, both personally and professionally. This is doubly true when handling internal candidates. Communicating the idea that "not today" doesn't mean "never" is important. Make the effort.

At the end of the day, hiring isn't the end goal. Selection identifies who can perform the tasks but becoming a qualified team member is a different challenge. How we support this through training matters to success at both the individual and brewery-wide level.

ORIENTATION AND TRAINING

Having a new employee is not the same thing as having a fully qualified operator on the team. To prepare people to succeed, it is worthwhile investing in a formal training program. Ad hoc training methods can suffice in many cases—breweries of all sizes do it every day, after all—but this style leaves the door open to errors and misunderstandings. There is a point at which "watch what I do, and you'll figure it out" stops being a workable path, even in small brewery settings.

Brewing has gone through many organizational models, each with its own training styles. Long before the modern period, beer was made at home by alewives, and techniques were passed from mother to daughter in the home. As brewing became professionalized (and women were largely blocked from participating in the industry), many areas saw the creation of variations on the guild model, where training followed the apprentice/journeyman/master pattern. Training started through rote learning and manual labor, and apprentices were largely told what to do with minimal explanation of the underlying concepts. Only later would more advanced concepts be incorporated, slowly indoctrinating trainees into the "mysteries" of their craft.

Later, the drive to understand the actual science underlying time-honored brewing techniques led to the creation of brewing schools and educational

programs. Breweries developed internal training programs, which were similar to the earlier apprenticeships, and promising candidates for advancement would be sent to programs such as TUM Weihenstephan, the Siebel Institute of Technology, and Heriot-Watt University to systematically learn the theory behind their practice. This training model operated for decades, and organizations like the Master Brewers Association of the Americas (MBAA) flourished, with education central to their mission. Large, multinational breweries still operate with this model, developing staff through highly structured on-the-job training and the provision of advanced training opportunities.

The rapid expansion of breweries in the modern era has created a new series of challenges. The rise of craft breweries in 1980s America was driven by the home-brewing movement, which was largely self-taught. Small breweries often lacked the resources to build formal internal training programs. The sense of craft brewing being a counterculture movement also led to a general lack of respect between the microbrewery movement and the larger, more corporate brewing community. Many craft brewers viewed industrial breweries as pure factories that didn't have any real lessons to teach them, while the intrepid craft brewer who attended a local district MBAA meeting in the mid-1980s was met with bemusement by veterans of the larger regional and national breweries who had grown up in those chapter meetings.[1]

Fortunately, the industry has developed stronger bonds across these various scales of operation. The current environment is more integrated, with a much broader range of conferences, brewing programs, and other educational opportunities. But lack of resources is still a reality for small breweries, and not just in terms of finances and cash flow; in most training scenarios, the most precious resource is time. This doesn't mean that smaller breweries don't train their staff—of course they do. However, this training is still largely informal in nature. Although new hires typically go through a job-shadow phase with a more experienced brewer, which is important, they are frequently released to work solo without any in-depth assessment of their readiness to operate on their own. Instead of spending time, money, and attention at the beginning of the process, these resources get consumed over a much longer time horizon as training deficiencies become apparent.

Training people, even when performed ad hoc, takes time and requires a considerable investment. This presents a challenge for breweries of every size, but one that hits particularly hard for smaller breweries that have limited staff. When hiring is performed in reaction to someone leaving, there is a drive to fill positions as swiftly as possible and get the new person onto the floor as quickly as possible. This drive is entirely understandable, but it is worth remembering that the goal isn't to fill gaps on an organization chart: you're trying to effectively perform the tasks that the org chart position represents. Performing a task isn't the same as performing a task correctly, and the difference is *training*. Developing training programs comes with a cost, but the results of an effective training system are well worth it.

The financial cost of dumping a single batch of beer may hurt, especially in the short term, but a poor training system will have a much more damaging effect if weaknesses become endemic and institutionalized. The reputational cost of poor customer service or bad beer in the market, whether at retail or at the distributor level, has a significantly longer half-life than the immediate consequences of a single incident. Problems involving safety or harassment in the workplace can result in costs far in excess of direct financial losses. These are fundamentally problems of organizational culture, not policy. Safety

EDUCATION VERSUS TRAINING

Educational opportunities for brewers have increased dramatically over the past decade. Many universities and community colleges have established programs specifically tailored to brewing. The majority offer a certificate in brewing operations, although some programs grant degrees. There has been a corresponding increase in job postings that list this type of education as an expectation for an ideal candidate. These programs are designed to provide a baseline understanding of brewing theory and expose students to its practical applications.

While educational programs provide students with a jumpstart in understanding areas such as mash enzyme chemistry, cleaning and sanitation protocols, and laboratory techniques, there is an argument for experience being the best teacher. The practical application of knowledge is the heart of internal training programs. Properly designed and implemented, these internal programs focus on teaching people how to do the daily realities of the job; the theoretical underpinnings can come later.

The reality is that both approaches work. After several years on the job, the differences tend to wash out. New hires with academic training still need an investment in practical training, while on-the-job trainees can learn the theoretical components of brewing over time. The important thing for brewery leadership is to make sure that orientation and training programs cover all aspects of the job description.

and harassment policies are meaningless if they don't go beyond a boilerplate policy and become the lived experience of staff throughout the brewery. Addressing these areas from the get-go prevents problems from becoming embedded in your organizational culture.

1 If you picture how homebrewers are often viewed by their commercial peers at conferences, you have a sense of the reception that craft brewers received in some MBAA district meetings. And so the wheel turns . . .

28

Establishing a common base of knowledge is central to unlocking the potential of every new hire. The whole point of the selection process was to identify people who can advance the brewery through their skills, experience, and viewpoints. This is essential to integrating candidates with diverse backgrounds, as well as for adapting the work habits of brewery industry veterans. The key to this transition will be developing a robust program of orientation (sometimes known as *onboarding*) and training. Different departments and roles will have their own specific needs, but you can identify a set of common themes. *Orientations* are intended to provide new employees with a functional understanding of their work environment and establish the brewery's priorities. *Training cycles* should be designed to carefully and deliberately introduce employees to the tasks and operations required by the position and provide a path toward competence.

ORIENTATION: SETTING THE TABLE FOR SUCCESS

The orientation phase comprises four primary sections: fundamentals, regulatory compliance, job shadowing, and a history component that explores the identity of the brewery. Having a basic onboarding checklist helps ensure that all of these are covered for each new employee. Once you have committed to holding an orientation, there is a temptation to pile every topic into a single session or single week. This approach is not particularly effective: there is just too much information to absorb and not enough context to genuinely understand the material being presented. It is a lot to learn in the first several weeks and months, much less a single day or week. Pacing this material over time is key. The goal should be to provide enough information for a new employee to operate safely in their assigned workspace while they go through the on-the-job training phase, as well as give them a general overview of the brewery as whole. There will be plenty of time to get into the details as the employee learns their craft.

Fundamentals

Fundamentals, as the name suggests, should cover the basics of being an employee at the brewery. This can be included in an employee manual, but taking time to talk through these components early and often will help ease the transition for new employees.

Table 2.1 **Fundamentals: Paperwork and orientation information**

Basic HR paperwork	Mandatory forms: I-9, W-4, etc.
	Payroll/benefits
	Emergency contacts and workers compensation insurance requirements
"Faces and spaces"	Introduce new employees to other members of the team, especially those who will serve as resources over their first weeks and months.
	Make a point of showing new employees important locations in the brewery, including, but not limited to
	• employee entrances and parking,
	• restrooms, break rooms/meal areas, and
	• a basic safety-focused walkthrough of the space.
	These sound obvious, but it is easy to overlook the obvious when the brewery gets busy and there is the temptation to get new hires working as quickly as possible.
Navigating the environment	Conflict resolution: This may seem like starting out on a negative note, but emphasizing and discussing it right away shows that problems will be taken seriously. Making it clear that there is an avenue for discussion and resolution is an act of confidence, not negativity.[a]
	Timecard procedures for punching in and out
	Procedures for calling in sick
	Getting a shift beer, using employee discounts, and other staff benefits
	Meal breaks: nearby coffee/lunch spots, rules for the employee refrigerator, etc.
[a] Whether the conflict resolution process leads to genuine action and change is a separate issue.	

Regulatory Compliance

Working in a brewery brings a variety of federal and state regulatory requirements that need to be communicated to employees in a time-sensitive manner. The most significant are worker safety requirements and food safety rules.

There are multiple components of the Occupational Safety and Health Act relating to workplace safety (29 C.F.R. § 1910) that affect breweries. Several pieces are best addressed early. Hazard communication, 29 C.F.R. § 1910.1200 (2021), is intended to provide employees with an understanding of the safety hazards and associated controls present in the workspace. Employers are obligated to train new employees on these hazards and maintain records of that training. Common hazards encountered in a brewery setting are outlined in table 2.2.

No hazard communication presentation or set of safety policies will cover every potential scenario, which is why the Occupational Safety and Health Act also contains the General Duty Clause:

Each employer shall furnish to each of his employees employment and a place of employment which are free from recognized hazards that are causing or are likely to cause death or serious physical harm to his employees. (29 U.S.C. § 654a(1) (2022))

Effectively, this states that employers have an obligation to protect their employees from harm while on the job. The next subsection completes the circle: employees also have an obligation to follow safety regulations (29 U.S.C. § 654b). Communicating this early on is an important commitment to the relationship between brewery and an employee, and it deserves to be highlighted during the orientation phase.

Training on more detailed, task-specific safety issues, such as lockout/tagout (LOTO), confined space entry, or operating a forklift, are better suited to later in the training process. Covering any more than the basics in orientation makes it difficult for new employees to absorb and retain information. Remember, the purpose of a safety orientation isn't to make them experts: the goal is to provide the information and awareness needed to operate safely in the brewery space on a day-to-day basis. A useful set of resources for the orientation phase is the Online Safety Video Training series from the Brewers Association. These are organized by topic as well as functional work area, plus they have short quizzes that can be used to document completion and comprehension of each assigned module. Other resources include the MBAA Toolbox Talks from the Master Brewers Association of the Americas, a series of short training pieces dedicated to individual topics and designed to be presented during staff meetings or pre-shift team huddles.

The last safety-related piece needed during orientation is how to communicate that something has gone wrong. If employees don't understand how to report safety issues, or don't feel empowered to do so, those issues will remain unresolved and the risk of injury will escalate. An easy way to communicate expectations around reporting safety issues is to categorize reporting into three tasks:

- Reporting a safety issue, such as a loose or missing piece of machine guarding

Table 2.2 **Common Hazards in the Brewery**

Alcohol / substance abuse	High voltages
Carbon dioxide	Hot liquids and surfaces
Chemicals (corrosive and oxidizers)	Lockout/tagout (LOTO)
Confined spaces	Mechanical equipment and guarding
Dock and warehouse safety	Milling and dust control
Elevated work platforms	Occupational noise
Ergonomic and repetitive motion issues	Pressurized vessels
Forklifts and other industrial lifts	Slips, trips, and falls

- Reporting a safety incident, such as a kettle boilover or forklift collision
- Reporting a work-related injury, such as a burn or pinch/crush injury

The importance of educating production and tap room employees on food safety issues follows a similar arc. According to the Food Safety Modernization Act, employees involved in working with food or food-contact surfaces need to be trained in their responsibilities to maintain a food-safe environment (21 C.F.R. § 117.4).

FYI

EMPLOYEE TRAINING REQUIREMENTS OF THE FOOD SAFETY MODERNIZATION ACT

Breweries need to develop and implement training programs that educate employees on the core concepts involved with food safety issues (Pellettieri and Nicholas 2020, 59–61). Training topics include:

- An overview of food safety
- Allergen handling
- Good Manufacturing Practice (GMP) requirements
- Cleaning and sanitation programs—food safety implications
- Personal hygiene requirements for a food facility

Training records need to be stored for a minimum of two years.

Job Shadowing

Following an experienced operator during orientation is an important tool for helping people acclimate to a new working environment. Allowing a new hire to simply observe operations for a few shifts before being assigned specific job duties provides context and helps them learn names and terminology, figure out where things are located, and understand how tasks fit together. For those who have never been in the industry before, this process is of immense benefit, helping to put them in a position where they can focus on the upcoming training process, rather than trying to figure out fresh jargon and what's happening around them while simultaneously having to do the job. Even for someone who has worked in breweries before, this approach helps to clarify differences between previous brewery jobs and their new one in your brewery.

Who you select to be those initial trainers or guides genuinely matters. They serve as the first point of contact for a new employee. One of the core functions of the job shadow phase is to emphasize the values of the brewery, so the guide needs to represent those values and be a positive example of how a job is performed. Doing a task is different from doing a task correctly, and it is important to demonstrate the standards expected of staff.

Managers are a common choice for the role, the reasoning being that they are, by definition, leaders. But managers often aren't a good fit for job shadowing because a manger's core responsibility is running the floor, not working at a specific station. Connecting a new hire with one or more experienced operators who have both the time and temperament to provide that first impression makes a genuine difference.

Job shadowing doesn't need to last very long. A shift or two will often suffice. Equally important, it shouldn't take the experienced operator's attention away from their normal duties. This isn't expected to be in-depth training: the goal is literally as simple as letting a new hire get a sense of the rhythm of the workspace before they have to focus on learning their own specific job duties and tasks. It also doesn't need to happen all at once; again, pacing matters. Providing a job-shadowing opportunity before starting to learn a new machine or process can be valuable for an employee even after their formal orientation period is over.

History and Identity

A central theme of any onboarding program involves fostering a sense of accountability with employees. Communicating a sense of history and identity is an important component of this process. Offering a new hire a connection to the past helps to provide a path for seeing themselves as part of the future. This component of orientation may not feel as concrete as the previous three, but it pays dividends over the long term. You can't force someone to feel pride in and a sense of connection or belonging to their workplace, but you can provide the background needed to begin creating that connection. Unless the fresh employee is already immersed in the local beer scene, it is unlikely that they know the history of your brewery or the parts you feel are central to your story. Make time to familiarize a new hire with the brewery's history, story, and beers. Just as breweries invest in telling their story to consumers through marketing and messaging, there are benefits to doing the same with employees through training.

This also doesn't have to be a complex process: if your brewery offers tours, assign a new hire to go on one or two tours during their first few weeks and then follow up with them to answer questions or provide additional details. Another option could be to host a monthly extended tour specifically for new employees. This can be tailored to new staff, digging into history and important facets of the brewery you want to highlight. It also presents an opportunity to begin educating new staff on the flavor profiles of your beers.

BRAND AND FLAVOR TRAINING

Brand and flavor training is useful for every position within the brewery, including production, taproom, and sales. While there is the temptation to teach off-flavors, this puts the cart before the horse: employees need to understand what the beers are *supposed* to taste like. A beer can be delicious and still not be true to the brand.

Tips and techniques
- Use written flavor guides
- Hold guided tastings of core brands
- Control new employees' shift beer selections for the first few weeks: devote each week to a different core beer so that they can really get to know the flavor profiles

Note that being an evangelist for the organization is neither necessary nor sufficient: the expectation is to prepare an employee who contributes to the whole organization, not create a superfan. Passion and incompetence are not a good combination. Some employees will just want to come to work, do their job, and then punch out at the end of the day. And that's OK. People have their own lives to lead—expecting their personal and professional worlds to merge is both unrealistic and unnecessary. What you want to cultivate is a work culture that demands (and then rewards) accountability in the workspace and offers opportunities to fully engage with the beer scene as desired.

The orientation phase should also make it clear that mistakes will happen and are an expected part of the process. Making an error is OK, if the person learns from it. Trainees who remain afraid to make mistakes tend to become risk-averse and begin to either avoid tasks outright or delay actions they know how to perform until someone else validates what they already knew to do. The message you want new employees to understand is that the learning process isn't about the mistakes themselves: it's about adapting and making the necessary corrections. Putting a new hire into a position where they could make a mission-critical failure is a leadership error, not an operator error. This dynamic changes as the trainee gains skills, but the core idea behind a training cycle is the gradual development of skills and the confidence that comes with that. Even when you are in the position of throwing a novice into the proverbial deep end of the pool to learn to swim, there shouldn't be an expectation of having them immediately serve as a lifeguard. The skill sets and confidence simply aren't there yet.

The flip side to becoming risk-averse is becoming indifferent to errors. Complacency is as big of a risk to the brewery as task-avoidance. Fundamentally, this is also a sign of a leadership problem, but the time to address this with new team members is early in the process. Educating employees on the costs and consequences of mistakes is important. Again, the point isn't to scare them: it is to be open and honest about how their work affects the process, their team, and the wider organization.

An important aspect of onboarding programs is that *time-sensitive* topics aren't necessarily *time-intensive*. The entire point is to help arm new employees with enough information to prepare them for a successful training experience. While there is a lot to cover in a thorough orientation, not everything will happen or needs to happen in the first day or even first week. There are items that need to be addressed straightaway, such as the "spaces and faces" portion (table 2.1), but topics such as safety will be an ongoing process. The amount of safety information that a new employee needs varies based on duties, workspace, and brewery environment. Certifying them on a forklift in the first week is a solid goal, but the priorities need to be hazard awareness and a commitment to safety as a core principle.

The in-depth training that will qualify a new employee for more advanced duties can wait until they have spent more time in their new role. This may take place during their second week or even later in their training cycle, as long as the employee isn't being asked to operate above their skill and certification level in the meantime. Areas such as detailed sensory profiles and brewery history can be inserted as schedules allow. It's important to cover these topics, so you don't want to wait too long, but attempting to cram everything into one week is akin to asking new employees to drink from a firehose. You're better off treating this as an opportunity for professional development and dosing in this material over time.

LAYING THE GROUNDWORK: BUILDING OUT A TRAINING PROGRAM

A key aspect of the orientation phase is to provide a sense of context around brewery operations and the entirety of the brewing process. This helps prevent the creation of "us versus them" silos between departments or work groups. There is no part of a brewery that operates well for very long unless every part is functioning well. There simply aren't any unimportant jobs, just undervalued ones. One of the goals behind job shadowing is to take this idea directly among their immediate co-workers: everyone contributes to the whole.

Preparing for the next phase involves providing the materials a new employee will need to learn their trade. This is where you introduce standard operating procedures (SOPs) and reaction plans, establish good habits early, and address bad habits as soon as they are recognized. Remember, your brewery is not the new hire's last employer in disguise, even if that previous employer was also a brewery. Confusion between new and old environments can lead to unnecessary errors: specifics matter, even when the fundamentals are the same. The basic principles are the same for every brewery, but individual layouts and valve configurations will vary, requiring operators to understand the

nuances of the current system. Even when equipment is identical, the process needs of your brands won't necessarily be the same as those the new employee used to work on. How you transition newly hired staff into their roles will drive the long-term success of both the individual operators and their teams.

You also want to explain why a task matters and how it fits into the overall picture. This is critical for morale. When tasks feel like busywork or pointless extra steps, it becomes hard to invest time and energy into them. Understanding the reasons behind an action provides essential context. It's equally critical for operations: people can't diagnose problems if they don't understand how equipment or processes are supposed to work.

Skills Progression Checklists

Just like the selection process started with an assessment of what skills you're looking for in a new employee, the preparation for a training program starts with the creation of a list of required job skills and knowledge for each position. This list should answer the question, "What does an operator need to know in order to be successful?" This is an opportunity to establish your priorities: as we've said before, priorities are either a lived experience or they aren't. Emphasizing these priorities must start early and then be maintained throughout the work experience.

The most straightforward way to sequence a training cycle is to lay out a calendar and mark down the skills a trainee will be expected to know at the end of each week. Everything else will be based on this schedule. Note that breweries aren't classrooms and lessons aren't delivered in neat 50-minute sessions. Trainees will be exposed to a wide variety of tasks and experiences every week while they are actively working. The point behind sequencing is that people are only going to be held accountable for the material scheduled for that week. If they pick up additional skills ahead of schedule, that's great, but it shouldn't be the expectation. Allowing new operators to focus on a relatively small set of tasks and skills at any given moment helps to prevent them from being overwhelmed by new information.

Another important feature of a skills progression checklist is making sure that the full range of work duties are captured during the training process. One of the downsides of training new people during day-time shifts is that certain tasks mainly occur during other shifts. Others just don't happen often and can easily get skipped over without a checklist to track the trainee's progress. Taproom operations have specific challenges along these lines. Most taproom staff don't work 40-hour weeks, so timing these training cycles isn't as routine as it would be for full-time staff. Again, this is where structure plays a role.

One simple way to begin a skills checklist is to refer back to the list of essential duties from the job description (p. 11). If those are what you expect from your staff, it makes sense that you ensure that each of those tasks is covered during the training cycle. How you sequence that progression will vary between work teams and can even be affected by seasonal changes in the pace of operations. The calendar schedule laid out at the start will guide the progression. If there are training areas that haven't been covered, then you need to find opportunities to provide that knowledge or recognize that a new employee won't be ready to perform certain tasks yet.

To use a production example, if you imagine an eight-week training cycle for new hires, you can establish a series of milestones. Week 1 will be devoted to orientation. The next several weeks will be built around two-week training blocks, each with their own set of training objectives. Weeks 7 and 8 can then be focused on covering material that needs extra attention and skills assessments for each of the assigned tasks. Taproom staff can build out a similar concept based on designating training objectives for each of an employee's first several shifts. The Brewers Association has a *Beer Server Training for Brewpubs* manual developed by the Brewpub Subcommittee. The manual, resource list, and blank templates are available for free on the association's website.

Table 2.3 Example Sequencing Schedule for Cellar Operations

Week	Objectives	Example details
1	Orientation	Admin components; safety; job shadowing
2	General Operations	Start-up procedures; storage locations; Good Manufacturing Practice; task-specific safety; process and instrumentation diagrams
3–4	General Operations	Process logs; QA/QC measurements; fermentation profile details; tank and hose setup/breakdown; cleaning and sanitation
5–6	General Operations	Sensory; dry-hopping; clarification and carbonation; yeast management
7–8	Competency Review	Provide time for repetition and practice, remedial training; determine whether operator is ready for solo operations

Table 2.4 Example Sequencing Schedule for Taproom Staff

Shift	Objectives	Example details
Orientation	Admin components; scheduling; tour the space	Handbook, ID policy, performance expectations; scheduling process; tour and guided beer tasting
1	Shadow the training lead: listen and learn	Emphasis on checklists and learning about the beers, glassware, history, etc.
2	Shadow the training lead: work on hands-on tasks	Working the register, side work, and delivery order system
3	Take the lead on service with training lead as backup	Opening or closing tasks; take point with customer interactions
4	Take the lead on service with training lead as backup	Additional training on receiving deliveries, tours and private events, and emergency procedures
Check-ins	30- and 90-day feedback; 1-year review	Go over what is going well, where they may be struggling, and answering questions

Standard Operating Procedures

Once you understand our training priorities and general timelines, you can develop training materials that address those requirements. Standard operating procedures (SOPs) are a good starting point. It is easy to think of these as a list of steps that need to be performed to do a task, but that misses the mark. At their core, SOPs are a *series of objectives*. Instead of focusing on the specific steps involved in a task, the function of an SOP is to explain what you're trying to achieve. The steps will document the actions needed, but the key lesson in every SOP is communicating the big picture before describing a set of best practices for a specific application. The SOP for running a 260 can-per-minute filler and the SOP for a benchtop crowler machine will have very different procedural steps, but the expectations and objectives are the same. Regardless of equipment, the filling process needs to meet the following criteria:

1. Operator safety requirements
2. Sanitary technique to prevent beer spoilage
3. Satisfy food-safety requirements
4. Minimize dissolved oxygen pickup
5. Ensure container integrity
6. Maximize efficiency and minimize waste

The rest of the document are just details that explain how to achieve those goals. The Brewers Association has a guide to creating SOPs,[2] and another is included in appendix G.

There are three broad types of standard operating procedure: basic step-by-step guides, training SOPs, and operational checklists. Step-by-step SOPs are how most standard operating procedures start and are built around a sequential narrative of how to perform a given task. They generally don't provide much in the way of context, but they offer an important starting point when developing a training program. Taking the time to document what is happening in the brewery is the first step toward accountability: people are either following the SOPs or they aren't, which drives behavior towards accountability.

Training SOPs are intended specifically as teaching tools and should go into depth when describing how to perform a task. Instead of simply describing a series of actions, they will assume minimal prior knowledge so that they are accessible to trainees regardless of experience and background. Including images and descriptions is incredibly helpful for trainees to help them orient themselves and follow along as they observe and learn new tasks. Training SOPs take more time to develop, but they offer significant

Figure 2.1. A large-scale can filler and a benchtop crowler filler. Despite the differences in scale and complexity, the basic objectives are the same.

2   Quality Subcommittee, *Standard Operating Procedures Guidance for Brewers* (Boulder, CO: Brewers Association, May 29, 2020), https://www.brewersassociation.org/educational-publications/standard-operating-procedures-guidance-for-brewers/.

advantages over basic guides. Going into greater depth gives trainees a better picture of not only what steps to take, but what outcomes they should expect from those steps—what is supposed to happen next and, critically, what the indicators of a problem look and sound like. When everything is working as intended, brewery work is fairly straightforward. But working in breweries is an exercise in dealing with situations where tasks don't go as intended, and the better each operator understands their responsibilities, the better prepared they are and the more effective the entire organization will be.

Both step-by-step and training SOPs formats share some common key features. First, they need to define the *what*, *why*, and *how* of a process or task. They should be operator-driven, rather than imposed from the top down. Experience from multiple industries has pointed to the same lesson involving training: efforts to dictate every step from the center will fail. Instead, the more effective path is to listen to the wisdom of the group. Whether in the taproom, on the production floor, or out in the field, your operators are the ones closest to what is happening. As described in the introduction, there is enormous value in giving people the power to make changes (Gawande 2009, 49, 67, 72–73).

Standard operating procedures also need to establish best practices. Just because a task is currently being done one way, it doesn't mean that's the correct way, much less the best way. The term "best practices" is a very deliberate choice. Again, the main goal of an SOP is to communicate key objectives, not carve a list of steps in stone. There are often multiple ways to accomplish a given task and still achieve the necessary objectives. Allowing people to have a measure of freedom when possible will make it a lot easier in the long term to implement a strictly defined set of steps when they're genuinely needed.

As your brewery grows and circumstances change, your SOPs need to reflect that. Effective SOPs are dynamic in nature and need to be integrated with a broad range of requirements. These include safety hazards and expectations, Good Manufacturing Practice (GMP) compliance, and (occasionally) legal obligations. Exactly where this information appears in the SOP will vary depending on your chosen format and the context.

EXAMPLE OF A MNEMONIC-BASED STANDARD OPERATING PROCEDURE

In emergency medical situations, first responders use a mnemonic called SAMPLE to help them remember to collect relevant information that guides diagnostic and treatment decisions. This tool helps emergency services personnel operate in a stressful situation without missing potentially critical information.

S: Signs and symptoms—what can you observe or measure, and when did they start?
A: Allergies—does the patient have any allergies that can either indicate a condition or guide medication?
M: Medicine—does the patient take any medications, and have they taken them recently?
P: Previous history—does the patient have any known medical conditions?
L: Last oral intake—how recently has the patient eaten, and what was it?
E: Event—what was the patient doing when symptoms began?

Operational checklists have a very different function. Instead of listing every step in a process or diving deep into the details, checklists will focus on the overall objectives and distill the steps into a series of reminders for the items that have the most impact on success. A classic example would be the pre-flight and landing checklists that pilots use. The point isn't that pilots don't remember how to fly a plane. Rather, pilots fly so often that it becomes easy to lose track of whether a task has been completed in the current instance versus accidentally remembering one of the hundreds of times that they've done a task previously. Having to actively track repetitive tasks can become confusing and exhausting over time, resulting in accidents.[3] Breweries possess similarly repetitive tasks. How many times have you or your team prepared a bright beer tank for a transfer in the past

---

[3] The genesis of pre-flight checklists was a fatal crash involving a highly experienced test pilot who overlooked a task during takeoff (Gawande 2009, 32–34).

month? Closed down the taproom at the end of the night? Or had to perform the nemesis of every brewery employee with a company credit card: submitting your expenses at the end of a billing cycle? Each of these procedures has critical steps that become routine through repetition, but they compete for attention with other activities. Operational checklists are intended to create reminders and pause points for routine tasks, allowing active mental bandwidth to be available for other tasks.

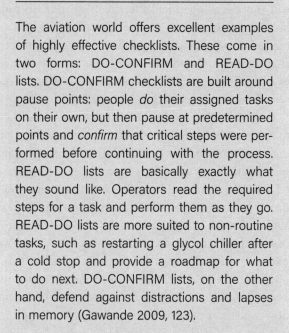

TYPES OF OPERATIONAL CHECKLIST

The aviation world offers excellent examples of highly effective checklists. These come in two forms: DO-CONFIRM and READ-DO lists. DO-CONFIRM checklists are built around pause points: people *do* their assigned tasks on their own, but then pause at predetermined points and *confirm* that critical steps were performed before continuing with the process. READ-DO lists are basically exactly what they sound like. Operators read the required steps for a task and perform them as they go. READ-DO lists are more suited to non-routine tasks, such as restarting a glycol chiller after a cold stop and provide a roadmap for what to do next. DO-CONFIRM lists, on the other hand, defend against distractions and lapses in memory (Gawande 2009, 123).

Note that operational checklists don't explain any of the actual steps: the knowledge of how to perform each component of a task is assumed. These are tools that come into play after the basics of a procedure have been learned. They are only there to communicate the minimum necessary steps. As a result, they should be precise and practical, with a limit of five to nine items being a good rule of thumb (Gawande 2009, 36–39, 120). For lists longer than that, the traditional step-by-step SOP format is more appropriate.

KEY FEATURES OF A STANDARD OPERATING PROCEDURE

- Defines the *who, what, why,* and *how* of each task
- Operator-driven
- Establishes best practices
- Dynamic in nature
- Integrated with safety, GMP, quality, and other requirements

Table 2.5 **Writing Process for SOPs**

Task	Assignment / Resources
Develop a common template: these help provide continuity across the organization	Leadership or HR / Online formats or professional groups
Define the scope: explain the task and objectives	Leadership / Department Leads
List the actions and steps	Written or driven by operators
Collect best practices and edit the document	Team review with operators and leaders
Plan for reviews	Team review

Corrective Measures and Reaction Plans

While SOPs are designed to get tasks done correctly, the reality is that things can still go awry. That may be because of operator error or through straightforward equipment malfunctions. Either way, they will need operator intervention to get back on track. Training operators on how to resolve problems is an important aspect of a successful organizational culture. Individuals become more confident and resilient and organizations are stronger when lanes of communication are open. You want people to be prepared to work through situations where things aren't going as expected and understand the difference between when to intervene directly and when to get help.

These interventions come in two forms. Corrective measures are real-time adjustments you make while in an active process.[4] An everyday example would

---

[4] In QA/QC circles, the phrase "corrective actions" is common. However, this phrase has a very different meaning in a performance management context. To avoid confusion, this book will use the term "corrective measures" to describe real-time adjustments.

be taste-testing a sauce in the kitchen. It may need adjustments to the salt level or to the level of thickening to reach the desired result. Recipes frequently just say "season to taste," which is useful but not particularly specific. Going the extra step and teaching people about balancing flavors, the properties of various herbs and spices, and then how to make adjustments as they go will generally lead to a tastier dish. Similar situations occur throughout the brewery setting. When titrating the chemical concentration for a clean-in-place (CIP) or sanitation cycle, the chemical solution may need more of the concentrate or need to be diluted to the correct level, just like adjusting the perception of salt in a sauce. Another common example involves carbonating a beer in a tank. If the carbonation is low, the corrective action is obvious: keep carbonating the beer. If the carbonation level is too high, however, the process for reducing carbonation while still protecting the foam-stable proteins is much more involved. Documenting these tasks and when to apply them and then including this information as an integral part of the training cycle helps prevent small errors from becoming significant problems.

Reaction plans are more involved and are tuned toward communicating effectively. While corrective actions happen at the individual level, reaction plans are defined step-action plans that address potential adverse events across teams. Step-action plans are designed to document in advance what needs to happen—they are effectively READ-DO checklists and are constructed the same way. The goal is to think through a process or task and anticipate potential problems:

- Who needs to be informed?
- What steps need to be taken? By whom and by when?
- Record actions and event details
- Provide for further investigation as necessary

A simple example of a reaction plan would be addressing a missed gravity target at knockout from the whirlpool. The first step involves recognizing it as a (solvable) problem. From there, the corrective action would typically involve adding or removing malt from the next grist bill, but that isn't always an option. You may need to blend the batch with an existing fermentation or even brew a follow-up batch specifically intended to even out the gravities. This will involve more people and can affect packaging timelines, both of which call for effective communication. Looking further out, more significant adjustments may be required to protect future brewhouse turns. This could be re-setting the mill roller gaps or making broad recipe changes to account for variances between malt lots.

A more involved example would be a glycol outage. If it is a simple maintenance issue, it will be resolved quickly and won't affect anyone else. However, the longer a glycol system is out of service, the further the ripples will spread through the brewery. Beer that can't be chilled can't be carbonated, and beer that isn't carbonated can't be packaged. At some point, the buffer space built into a production schedule will affect operations upstream and downstream. Sales can't do much with beer that is still trapped in a tank, and sooner or later the brewhouse will run out of open tanks for wort and have to stop brewing, which will also ripple through to sales eventually. Recognizing when a problem has the potential to affect other teams and *then communicating with them* is essential. Both corrective measures and reaction plans are prime candidates for flowcharts (Pellettieri 2015).

The preparation for on-the-job training takes a while to accomplish, but the development process is largely a one-time expense. This is why this chapter is spending so much time discussing developing training programs: ad hoc programs yield inconsistent results and still demand significant amounts of time for experienced staff during the training process. It is far more effective over the long term to invest this time up front. Training materials will still need to be periodically assessed and updated, when necessary, but once the materials are assembled, the bulk of your training time will be spent delivering that content to employees.

TRAINING CYCLES: WHERE THE RUBBER (FINALLY) HITS THE ROAD

Let's recap where you've got to: you've provided trainees with a broad understanding of the workspace through orientation and you've developed a set of training materials and corresponding schedule. Now you are ready to deliver that material. Once you are actively working with trainees, you have to deliver that information in a way that is accessible and attainable. An effective approach is through a series of progressive modules. This is often referred to as the "crawl, walk, run" model. Essentially, tasks are broken down into manageable chunks, starting with relatively simple concepts or tasks and slowly increasing the complexity until you approach real-life operational conditions.

The pacing for this progression isn't based on how quickly you can deliver the content. Instead, your goal needs to be maximizing retention. There is a considerable body of research about learning models that goes beyond the scope of this text, but an important insight is that being exposed to a topic is not the same thing as learning that topic. Genuine learning is an active process that has two pathways that need to be developed: bringing information in and then, critically, getting that information back out in a usable fashion.

What this means in practice is that job shadowing isn't enough. Trainees need to have opportunities to put information into practice. This can happen in a variety of forms. Even something as simple as taking notes during training helps to develop that active pathway, especially if the notes are rewritten later. A more hands-on approach would be to walk through a task and deliberately work through each individual step without the equipment or process being active. This helps build awareness and muscle memory while in a low-stakes situation that avoids the risk of consequential errors.

Depending on the individual, some trainees will rely more on the written SOP, while others will look to their trainers for verbal explanations or demonstrations. Understanding how people learn is a critical part of the training process. Note, this does not mean "learning style." While some people may have preferences between visual, auditory, reading/writing, and hands-on learning modes, the research literature doesn't support the use of one mode over another having a significant effect on results. Instead of tailoring delivery to a specific mode, mixing these approaches has been shown to deliver higher comprehension and retention rates.

Managing the level of complexity is important. Trainees need to experience tasks in a real-world operating environment, but there still needs to be time to absorb the material. Rushing the process will only lead to errors and frustration. Trainers need to exercise patience and be willing to repeat the same lessons multiple times depending on the learner. An effective strategy is to have them perform the walk phase of one task while starting the early phase of a related task (i.e., the "crawl" phase—these phases are discussed shortly). For example, a new person in the cellar can begin shadowing their trainer to learn the basics of operating a centrifuge while performing tank CIP or sanitation duties with much less supervision.

SELECTING TRAINERS

Teaching people is a specific skill and it is important to put some thought into who is selected to be a trainer. A common approach is to assign training duties to the most experienced team member or a manager. Neither of these is an inherently bad choice, but there are traps embedded in this approach. First, having experience is not the same thing as being skilled at communicating that experience. Effective trainers need to be able to explain tasks in ways that students can absorb, and these will vary from student to student. Flexibility and patience are the keys here, not experience. When there is confusion, a trainer should ask themselves whether they've made a lesson too complicated or used jargon without explaining it (McCord 2017, 21). Your experienced operators are the ones you want directly involved in writing SOPs, but they may not be your best choice for a trainer.

Managing people is also a specialized skill. Since they will be responsible for holding people to standards, it makes sense to task managers with training people to those standards. The problem is that managers have their own duties and aren't always the day-to-day operators. Pulling them away from their role in managing the overall team can be counterproductive and a recipe for micromanagement. A manager's time is best spent later in the process, during the assessment and evaluation phase.

The Crawl Phase: Developing Awareness

The starting point for learning any new task is to develop an understanding of the basic operating principles. Some of this was addressed during orientation: what does the space look and sound like when it is working correctly? Moving to the active training phase, you want to explain *why* things work the way they do as well as *how* to perform the task.

For example, you can teach someone the steps required to carbonate a beer, but the steps alone don't explain what is happening. Carbonation in beer is a balancing act between the beer temperature and the head pressure on the tank. Trying to carbonate a beer that is too warm is going to lead to frustration, no matter if the other steps were performed correctly. Similarly, a bartender with a tap line that is pouring with excessive foam is often tempted to look at the gas regulator as the accelerator on a car: if the beer is foamy, it would seem to make sense to lower the pressure at the regulator, but it's also the wrong corrective measure in most cases.

In this early phase of developing awareness, you want to concentrate on ensuring new employees understand the fundamentals and develop successful patterns, whether those are mnemonic devices and other memory aides, or actual muscle memory built up through practice and repetition. These memory devices may be acronyms, visual tags on equipment, or even rhymes that a trainee comes up with on their own to help remember important information. The point is to develop structures that help employees stay on track and not miss steps. Training SOPs are built around providing this material, but there are other techniques that can be used as well.

Practicing motor skills early and often is equally helpful. Maneuvering a clamp and gasket doesn't get easier when connecting a hot water line to a tank CIP arm or bending underneath a conical bottom to harvest yeast with sanitary technique. Providing trainees with plenty of practice in a low-stakes setting will help prepare them for more complex tasks later down the line by developing familiarity and muscle memory.

A key goal at this stage is to not overcomplicate a task. There are numerous ways in which a process can get off track, but there are limits on how much information a person can manage at any given time. People have a natural tendency to focus on the last pieces of information they're exposed to. Thus, instead of describing a rogue's gallery of what can go wrong, trainees will be better served when you emphasize a short list of factors that they can directly control to perform the task correctly. Focus the trainee's attention on what they should do, not what could go wrong.

Breweries are complex environments, so breaking down processes into manageable chunks is an important step. It pays to devote some time to helping trainees

to navigate the workspace. An example of this would be having them draw or trace the various fluid pathways in the brewery with process and instrumentation diagrams (P&IDs). A sample assignment for a trainee would be to hand them a basic drawing of the brewhouse vessels and then have them follow the pipes all the way from the grist hopper to the heat exchanger. From there, they can be tasked with placing visual tags on each valve and motor, while marking them on the diagram. All of these steps help define and build spatial awareness of the workspace, helping to establish not just where valves are but also how they are connected to the rest of the system. The same model can be used for filtration and other types of beer transfers, providing an opportunity to build up a new employee's mental map of the brewery before they move into the normal pace of work.

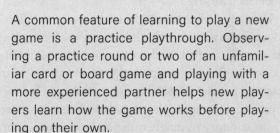

ANALOGY: GAME TUTORIAL MODES

A common feature of learning to play a new game is a practice playthrough. Observing a practice round or two of an unfamiliar card or board game and playing with a more experienced partner helps new players learn how the game works before playing on their own.

Many video games contain a tutorial at the beginning. Some are clearly defined as such, while others are built through a series of basic challenges that require the player to use various techniques at the beginning of the game. These are designed to familiarize a new player with the controls and game mechanics before embarking on the actual campaign or gameplay. Examples of common actions or indicators are progressively introduced to educate the player on what to do or look for in the actual game.

Job shadowing performs a similar function to a practice playthrough. Finding further opportunities to provide trainees with practice in a low-risk setting is a powerful tool.

Another useful tool is a "Controls and Sensors" session. These are particularly useful with filters, centrifuges, and packaging equipment, but the idea can be applied to virtually any system, including taproom environments, warehousing and inventory control, and even sales. The purpose of these sessions is to familiarize the trainee with how the equipment is designed to function, the controls that the operators can manipulate, and the various sensors that perform as signals or trigger actions. Having an opportunity to work through the machine functions slowly and deliberately makes it much easier for operators to make adjustments in real-time *before* problems become significant.

The Walk Phase: Gaining Competence

The end goal of the crawl phase is for a trainee to understand the fundamentals of a task and have a working familiarity with the actions necessary. Once a trainee can reliably find their way around their assigned area, you can dive into teaching them how to do the job. The focus needs to remain on the factors they directly control, but now is the time to begin addressing the complexities of the job.

Training with SOPs and corrective measures are integral to this, but so is the trainer. Ideally, you want new operators to work with an experienced employee. The combination of SOP and trainer is the key to trainees successfully gaining competence, and there are several stages to this process. The initial steps in the training process are intended to build awareness but understanding how the pieces of the puzzle fit together requires a guide.

First, you want new operators to follow along with the training SOP and actively ask questions. To genuinely develop proficiency, trainees need opportunities to regularly put knowledge into practice. It is very common for students to feel that a demonstration or lecture makes complete sense at first, only to find themselves confused later on. This is where providing a blend of training approaches is critical. Getting information into someone's head is only half the equation. Helping the person find ways to express that knowledge is the key to them being able to act on it later down the road. If a trainee is a note-taker by nature, give them time and space to write and rewrite them. If their comfort zone is being directly hands-on, facilitate opportunities to turn valves or otherwise interact with equipment while it's idle.

THE MIMIC MODEL

People naturally model their behavior based on what they see around them. This can be remarkably effective: children learn to speak a language purely through observation and usually have established an accent by the time they're three years old. Observation will only get them so far though: if you watch that same three-year-old brush their teeth, you will see a lot of activity with questionable effectiveness. They *think* they're doing great, but the actual coordination and awareness isn't there yet.

This is an example of the mimic model, and its weaknesses become more significant as tasks increase in complexity. Picture yourself driving a car down a busy street. Now ask yourself how much of your activity would be apparent to a 15-year-old sitting in the passenger seat. They may notice many of the active steps you take, such as turn signals and applying the brakes. They may even track your use of mirrors. What they can't directly observe are the judgement calls you make and, more importantly, the actions you *don't* take, so they aren't going to be capable of mimicking those behaviors unless you make a point of describing your thought processes. There is so much involved in driving a car that you have internalized, you don't even realize you're doing it until called on to actively explain it.

Brewing has similar challenges. Trainees will mimic what they see you do, but they won't be able to see the paths and choices you don't act on. That kind of experience is invisible to the mimic model and has to be delivered both through careful example and deliberate explanation. Your people are worth the investment.

The Run Phase: Establishing Proficiency

As a trainee's familiarity with a task increases, they'll rely less on directly reading the SOP or prompts from their trainer about what to do next. Moving forward, they can transition to operating with the trainer in the background letting them do as much as they can from working memory, with the SOP or trainer on standby in case there is a question on how to proceed. To use a theater analogy, actors start by reading their lines from a script, then move to having the script in hand as a reference, and then take the leap of leaving the script behind and delivering their lines from memory, with only the occasional prompt.

At this point, complexity becomes a critical teaching aid: over the long term, the best teachers are the challenges we face. Trainees need to operate semi-autonomously, with the trainer only stepping in to prevent safety or critical quality incidents. Having a set of operational checklists available will help to guide behavior and remind the trainees of the core objectives even when someone isn't looking over their shoulder.

Earlier in the training cycle, employees were allowed to concentrate on the basics of one task or work through functional training blocks in a limited number of areas. The run phase is where you allow the trainee to experience the full range of work duties and how they overlap. By having to move from one task to another, trainees get more practice in having to pull information from memory, improving their skills at problem-solving. This learning strategy, called *interleaving*, has been shown to develop better retention rates than studying information blocks alone (Pan 2015).

This may sound purely academic and complicated, but the truth is that moving through a variety of tasks throughout the day is basically just a normal day in the brewery. You laid the foundations in the crawl phase and practiced the mechanics of tasks during the walk phase. The run stage of training is entirely about allowing trainees to apply their new skills in the real-world environment. As the trainee gains experience, they learn how to adapt what they've learned to new situations.

ACCOUNTABILITY AND SKILLS ASSESSMENTS

As trainees approach the transitions from one phase to another for each of the assigned skills, it pays to measure their level of performance. Assuming that a candidate is ready for the next step based solely on the length of training or general observation carries numerous risks. In controlled settings, it is easy to

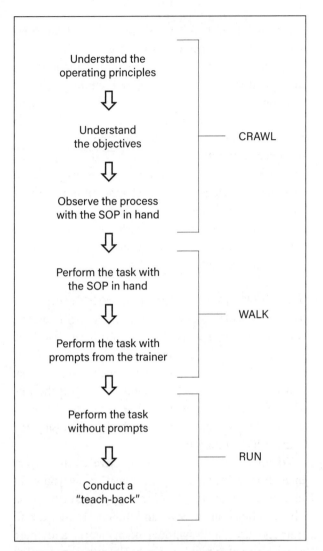

Figure 2.2. This figure illustrates an idealized path toward developing proficiency.

overestimate skill levels, both by the student themselves and by an observer.

The better route is to incorporate skills tests throughout the training progression. This has numerous advantages. First, employees gain confidence through demonstrated knowledge: there is a difference between a trainee thinking they understand something and proving they understand it. Second, leaders and managers can gauge performance and address the knowledge gaps that are identified and where more work is needed. The realities of the brewery can interfere with even the best-laid plans, no matter how well-developed a training cycle may be. Addressing knowledge gaps during the training pipeline is generally going to be preferable to having to deal with them later. There will absolutely be circumstances where learning certain skills won't fit into the available timeframe. That's perfectly fine: the point of training and assessment is to know what new employees *can* and *cannot* do, and then schedule them accordingly.

You also want to include challenge testing, especially on corrective measures and reaction plans. Explicitly ask the trainee to explain how they would make adjustments to a process. Another technique is to set up a series of simulated problems and have the trainee work through them. By providing challenge testing, you can evaluate how well a new staff member understands their responsibilities before having to find out the hard way.

Another very effective tool is a teach-back moment. This technique involves having the student teach the material back to the trainer, explaining a task while the trainer pretends to be a beginner. This is particularly effective at determining how well someone understands the fundamentals of a task. As we saw with the mimic model, a trainee can perform a task effectively under controlled circumstances without understanding what they're doing. This becomes a problem when they experience an unfamiliar situation.

TRAINING LEVELS

1. **Not trained**
2. **Exposed:** Can perform basic functions safely, but nothing else without clear direction
3. **Intermediate:** Can perform setup/cleanup and can handle basic troubleshooting during operations with minimal supervision
4. **Competent:** Can perform all aspects of the operation without supervision
   - Setup/cleanup
   - General operations
   - Troubleshooting
   - Corrective measures
   - Preventive maintenance
   - Reporting (as needed)
5. **Proficient:** As above, plus comfortable teaching the functions to new operators
6. **Mastery:** Can perform advanced troubleshooting and diagnostics

COMMANDER'S INTENT

Commander's intent is a concept that basically translates into defining the primary objective a team is trying to accomplish (Heath and Heath 2007, 26–28). Planning is essential, but situations can change and make the initial plan obsolete. However, if there is a clear understanding of what the goals are, teams can work out an alternative plan that yields the same results.

From a training and operations perspective, the commander's intent idea can be adapted for use in a brewery setting. If a company's values and expectations are well-defined, staff will understand what the main goals are in the event that something happens that isn't covered by existing training. This is particularly true during a training cycle: a new hire may not have been trained on a specific task yet, but real-world situations don't care who is on duty at the time. As long as the team's decisions are made in good faith, employees can make procedural errors without getting into trouble. The brewery's core values are more important than a specific policy or procedure. Example situations include stopping a process because of a safety or quality concern; taking a beer off tap if it doesn't taste right; and reporting problematic behavior.

A major aspect of managing accountability is knowing when to assess these skills. Just as you need to measure performance, you also need to manage the timing of those measurements appropriately. This goes back to the calendar schedule established during the training development phase (p. 33). A major part of that involved working out what you expect employees to know and when you need them to know it. It isn't reasonable to expect an operator to understand their entire range of duties within a few weeks, so establishing priorities will matter. Setting up a series of broad 30, 60, and 90-day expectations can help. The first 30 to 60 days can be broken down into a smaller set of training blocks (table 2.3), while leaving the later weeks open for flexibility.

PREPARING FOR THE LONG TERM: SKILLS RETENTION

No matter how effective a training program is, there will be certain skills employees have that need to be regularly maintained in order to keep them sharp. Day-to-day operations simply don't cover the full range of experiences that you want employees to be prepared to handle. This is particularly true with safety issues in the brewery: you want these incidents to be rare—nonexistent, in fact—but operators need to be prepared to react swiftly and accurately when they occur. In the US, some states require regular training on regulatory requirements,[5] but holding these sessions is a best practice in a much wider variety of situations regardless of regulatory requirements. There are two basic categories for skills maintenance: refresher training and reactive training.

Refresher Training

Refresher training is built around the idea that skills that are not routinely used still need to be maintained. In its most basic form, this refers to tasks that are rarely performed, such as fire drills and other emergency response plans. This model also applies to maintaining various certifications. For example, forklift certifications need to be renewed every three years, while taproom staff may be required to periodically go through alcohol service training and food safety education, depending on the jurisdiction. Looking more broadly, you can also address fundamentals through proactive reviews of SOPs. These sessions can include discussion of trends and updates to best practices.

Reactive Training

Reactive training works a bit differently to refresher training. These are sessions that are implemented in response to specific events. Safety incidents are a common example. Any time there is a forklift collision involving an injury or property damage, the federal code requires drivers to undergo retraining to maintain their certification. Another example is process change management: any time there is a change to a process, ingredient, or equipment, there should be a discussion of the safety and quality implications. If those affect operator behavior, then you need to arrange time to communicate that information to the team. Similarly, quality incidents can also trigger training sessions. These may happen at the individual or team level, but significant events require significant responses. Whatever the situation, these are opportunities to address problems and improve performance.

Recordkeeping

Documenting the training progression may seem like a minor point. After all, a consumer is only going to notice when a training issue causes a problem, not whether the training log was filled out. Having said that, documentation is an important part of accountability at several levels. Individually, they provide a record of the training each employee has received, showing where you can reasonably expect performance versus where you can't.

There are regulatory components that need to be satisfied that have repercussions for legal compliance and liability. In particular, Occupational Safety and Health Administration (OSHA) inspections operate under the presumption that if something isn't written down, then it didn't happen. While it is true that the content of a forklift training program is more important than the logbook documenting that training, maintaining the required documentation simply isn't a big ask. Just do it.

---

5   For example, at time of writing, this was the case for California and Minnesota.

PROFESSIONAL DEVELOPMENT

As was noted in the introduction, breweries are places of action, not static spaces. Sometimes change presents itself through increased demand and volume, leading to additional shifts, equipment, or facilities. In other cases, the brewery may expand into new business sectors, such as entering additional sales territories or introducing new product lines. Whether you're adding a package format or entering the event space and catering business, navigating new business opportunities will demand additional skills sets.

This can also happen when there are no plans for active growth: market forces don't stop evolving just because you have reached a specific milestone in your original business plan. Changing retail environments and shifts in consumer preferences are ever-present realities.

To protect the long-term viability of the brewery as a business, your teams need to evolve with those changes—you can't hire your way out of every challenge. There is a limit to what can be covered during the initial rounds of training, so you need to continually invest in your staff members over time and prepare them for the future by investing in technical proficiencies, software skills, and analytical capabilities. In the short term, you are going to be better prepared for operational growth. Over the long term, having critical skills distributed across individuals and teams supports employee morale and health by keeping staff from being overworked. Paid time off

and other benefits don't mean much when employees don't feel that they can genuinely use them.

The fundamental metrics we'll use to assess this investment are flexibility and versatility, that is, the measure of how adaptable your organization is to challenges across all phases of the business. To develop these capabilities, professional development offers three main avenues: cross-training, leadership development, and investing in advanced skills; the latter is ultimately beneficial for both individual employees and the brewery as a whole, as advanced skills increase an employee's potential for remuneration and can save the brewery's bottom line by reducing the number of tasks that have to be outsourced.

CROSS-TRAINING

Organizations are strengthened by having employees with at least a basic familiarity across multiple functional areas in addition to their regular area of expertise, and breweries are no exception. When critical information is limited to only a handful of people, the brewery is vulnerable to not being able to access that information in time-sensitive situations. It doesn't matter whether an employee is on sick leave, vacation, or no longer works for the company: if no one else remembers where to source a critical part for the brewhouse, use the back-up DE filter, or access the admin account for your point-of-sale system or social media accounts, life is about to become very frustrating and potentially expensive.

Cross-training isn't always seen as "professional development," but the advantages are significant. The most obvious increase in flexibility comes from the ability to absorb absences caused by illness or vacations, but there are more subtle items that play out on a daily basis. Something as simple as an operator stepping out for lunch can shut down a production line if there aren't people qualified to take over critical tasks. This has an immediate operational cost when it happens, but it also has a human cost when people feel that they *can't* walk away from a particular machine or process because there isn't anyone else who can perform the task. This quickly becomes draining and is unsustainable over the long term.

Day-to-Day Flexibility

The first step to cross-training is identifying where you need flexibility in handling daily workloads and tasks. Being able to cover short absences like restroom or meal breaks is generally straightforward and happens within a specific team (e.g., packaging or server table service). Managing this may be the end state of a well-developed training program, but you still need to put some effort into the process in order for it to go smoothly, especially when it is an unexpected event such as an employee calling out sick. As we saw in the evolution of training stages (chap. 2), being familiar with a task doesn't always equate to competency; developing skills through cross-training is important. Training and competency take time, so establishing a base level of experience and exposure across the entire team in advance pays dividends.

Longer absences, such as a vacation or having an employee on an injury-related work restriction, require some forethought in order to minimize disruptions. What skills are needed to maintain the expected level of safety and quality during operations? Exactly who was assigned to the brew deck, packaging line, or taproom opening shift on any given day shouldn't affect the customer experience. Some tasks will require specific expertise, such as specialized preventive maintenance procedures, but those aren't routine by definition: they can be scheduled around planned absences. The daily hurly-burly of the brewery is what you need to prepare for.

To achieve this, start by cataloging the competency levels within a team. Ideally, you want multiple people with expertise on any given piece of equipment or process.

A best practice approach would be to have three to four people rated as "Competent" (see p. 43), preferably with two of them assigned to the same shift. This allows for flexibility while still operating at a high level. Once you understand the skill levels present within a team, you can start cross-training other operators to serve as backups. Regularly rotating team members through tasks will aid in helping to maintain those skills.

You also have to prepare for what happens when a skilled operator is pulled away from an operation they're already doing. Transferring one person to cover an absence will naturally create a gap somewhere else. In a perfect world, a stable team will achieve mastery on every task in the brewery over time. Unfortunately, production demands and factors such as staff turnover present a challenge. Understanding the actual levels of competency across a team allows you to know which personnel you can shift between tasks while minimizing vulnerabilities. It also provides a road map to where you need to build additional expertise within the team.

That last point is important. In many cases, a manager can step in to cover a gap, but that also means that they aren't available to do other functions. This isn't always a sustainable option, so you want to develop capabilities more broadly across a team. In practice, this flexibility comes from developing broad proficiency within a team, understanding where there are crossover skills between teams that require minimal training to apply, and establishing options for rotating through tasks with the staff you have available. By recognizing where you need cross-trained employees, even if limited to the basics of a few tasks outside of an operator's normal role, you can dramatically increase their versatility.

Cross-Functional Flexibility

Departments or functional groups don't need to be a barrier to cross-training. The fundamental metric you'll use to assess this investment is flexibility. In fact, spreading expertise across groups can greatly simplify workflows and scheduling. The key is to look past traditional roles and responsibilities and avoid the tendency for gatekeeping. For example, training taproom staff on how to respond to a basic boiler alarm or start a hot liquor tank recirculation pump can save production staff from having to come in during off-hours. Addressing the safety issues for these tasks isn't any different than training a production brewer: it is solely a function of looking at teams more broadly and recognizing aptitude and attention to detail across the brewery. In small breweries, this frequently happens out of necessity, but it is always a useful practice, independent of scale. No one grows out of the need for versatility.

A prime example of this involves shipping and receiving duties. As much as we try to arrange for deliveries to arrive during specific time windows, that doesn't always happen. However, when a delivery truck shows up, exactly who is there to receive it shouldn't matter if they've been trained on what to look for. There is more involved than just signing the receipt slip. Is the material damaged? Does the delivery even match the bill of lading? Where does the material need to be stored in the brewery? Does it need refrigeration or contain an allergen? How does the receipt need to be documented? Conducting this level of training provides a valuable measure of flexibility for the brewery.

Sensory panels are another area that is ideally suited for broad participation. Limiting sensory evaluation to production staff is a recipe for trouble. Not every panel even needs to be technical: brand familiarization training sessions are invaluable in the taproom environment for identifying differences before they become consumer issues.

SENSORY TRAINING LIST

Sensory training is a complex and involved topic with multiple approaches. The following list offers a high-level look at areas to consider.

- Overview: Tasting technique
- Beer in process: Distinguishing between normal versus abnormal for actively fermenting beer
- Finished beer: Learning the target flavor characteristics for each brand and understand what qualifies as "true to brand"
- Advanced techniques:
  - Identifying off-flavors
  - Threshold training
  - Descriptive and diagnostic sensory panels
  - Comparative panels (e.g., triangle, duo-trio, etc.)
  - Designing sensory panels

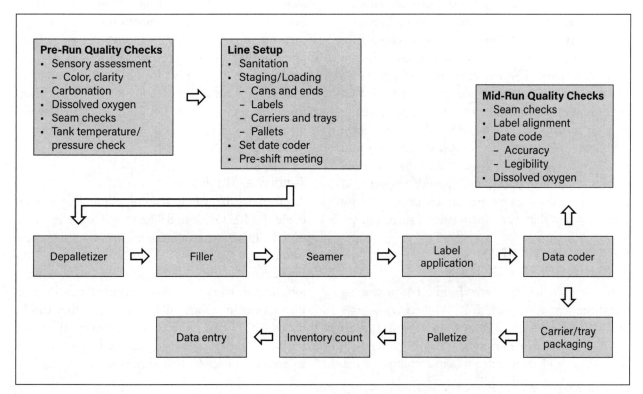

Figure 3.1. The range of tasks and duties involved in operating a canning line with pressure-sensitive labels.

Providing cross-training opportunities does more than facilitate operations in the brewery. It is also a useful way to identify people with the necessary aptitude and attention to detail to be viable internal candidates for future job openings, whether those are in production, sales, or management.

Recognizing and Appreciating Skills across the Brewery

An additional benefit from cross-training involves the broader concept of team building and morale. We'll explore this in greater detail later, but a challenge within every organization is the tendency for departments and groups to become silos, and breweries are no different. Providing opportunities for employees to spend a day in the shoes of another department can go a long way in counteracting this tendency. Here, your goal isn't to increase the functionality of the brewery or the flexibility of your teams. Instead, your aim is to build awareness about the work that the employees' peers do and reduce the tendency for an "us versus them" dynamic to develop.

Having staff trained and equipped to operate across departments has significant value for team dynamics, both during normal operations and when preparing for brewery changes over time, such as through expansive growth or normal staff turnover. Exposure to other tasks within the brewery reduces internal friction and the related rivalries that can develop. From a purely functional viewpoint, there is a case to be made that brewers and cellar staff need to understand what goes on in packaging and vice versa. Jessica Mellem, director of operations for The Tinley Beverage Company, points out, "It's not just putting cans and bottles in boxes. There is a wide skillset that is needed to be successful in packaging."[1] Mutual respect is at the core of positive team dynamics and helps to ensure that talent and skill aren't restricted to a single group.

LEADERSHIP AND MANAGEMENT SKILLS

Leadership comes in many forms, but managing teammates is a learned skill. As breweries grow and develop specialized teams, management skills become increasingly important. This is particularly true when production extends across multiple shifts.

Implementing an extra shift on a canning line isn't as simple as just hiring more people: smoothly meshing a group of individuals with all of their various skills and experiences into an effective team requires competent management. Beyond production, consider how both hospitality and packaging teams tend to become larger than their brewhouse and cellar counterparts; with this comes the need for developing team management skills.

Management Tracks

Management is a specific skill set: it isn't just the next level of advancement for a skilled employee. Providing guidance and education to build management skills is an important part of professional development. Mentorship from existing leadership is essential, but there are advantages to looking for outside training resources. This is something that military organizations recognized and have acted on for decades. As service members advance into certain roles or ranks, they are sent to specialized training programs designed to equip them with the required leadership and management skills.

The brewing industry doesn't have an arm specifically dedicated to professional management training, but there are resources available. We'll go into leadership and management in chapter 5, but know that the Brewers Association has a mentorship program, and there are programs available through universities and professional human resources organizations. Another avenue is to partner with your local chamber of commerce to network with other businesses and draw from their resources and experience. Management-oriented seminars are also increasingly featured at industry conferences.

Technical Tracks

Another way to invest in training and development on the leadership side is to deliberately develop technical experts. This becomes a valuable career track for people who are better with tasks than managing teams. They can be assigned specialist roles as subject matter experts for complex equipment or procedures, providing an internal resource for troubleshooting, or they can be tasked with special projects to support growth or help the brewery adapt to change. Technical experts are also an excellent choice for training new hires.

---

[1]   Quoted in Gary Nicholas, "Elevating Your Packaging Team," *New Brewer*, July/August 2021, http://onlinedigitalpublishing.com/article/Elevating+Your+Packaging+Team/4075054/714645/article.html.

ADVANCED SKILLS: RESOURCES AND STRATEGIES

Every form of professional development needs an avenue for delivery. Cross-training will generally be done on the job, but other skills will require you to look beyond the brewery's walls. Fortunately, there is a tremendous number of resources and opportunities available.

Giving employees an opportunity for professional development is an expenditure of resources, both in terms of direct financial costs and time away from the brewery. As with any expense, there needs to be a return on investment. How you calculate that can vary depending on the situation, but understanding and communicating the expectations in advance is the best practice for the brewery as an organization and for the individual employee. The key to success is not just realizing those opportunities for individual employees, you must then provide ways for the information to spread throughout the wider team and organization. The point is to get new information and insights into the bloodstream of the brewery. There's nothing wrong with sending people to conferences as a reward for performance, but not having a two-way flow of information is a missed opportunity.

One strategy is to require employees returning from a conference or course to write up their notes to share with others or to lead a discussion among their peers. Other strategies include tasking employees with researching information for a special project or have them take on responsibilities such as joining the safety committee, participating on brewery sensory panels, or operating as a staff trainer. The specifics will vary depending on the circumstances, but the leverage you gain from professional development opportunities comes from strengthening the overall brewery.

Conferences

Professional conferences tailored for the brewing industry have grown considerably over the years. The annual Brewers Association's Craft Brewers Conference® (CBC™) has grown from an event that fit into a handful of hotel rooms into a multitrack series of seminars and a trade show requiring an entire convention center.[2] The history of brewing conferences is much older, however. The Master Brewers Association of the Americas (MBAA), which has been convening annual conferences since 1887,[3] has a rich tradition of holding technical lectures at quarterly district meetings, as well as full-blown technical conferences such as the annual Technical Conferences held by District Ontario or District Rocky Mountains, among others.

Other organizations also provide valuable information, including the American Society of Brewing Chemists (ASBC), various state guilds, and international bodies such as the European Brewing Congress (EBC). Regardless of the host organization, there are significant advantages to approaching these conferences with a plan. There are multiple seminar tracks happening simultaneously, so attending every talk isn't an option for most breweries. You can prioritize what to attend by taking time to review the seminar list and compare those topics against your brewery's current or projected situation, but it is useful to leave space for individuals to make some of their own choices as well. In addition to providing space for personal growth and rewarding curiosity, it's valuable to be humble and recognize that tomorrow's challenges aren't always obvious today.

In addition to conference registration, conferences also require travel expenses, which can be significant even for large breweries. It's sometimes hard to pull people away from the brewery for multiple days, so attendance at these conferences is often limited to senior staff so as to maximize the accumulated experience of those walking the trade show floor and meeting with vendors. That can leave out staff who are just beginning their careers, but technical seminars at state guild meetings and local conferences provide more affordable avenues, with talks that are often directly aimed at brewing fundamentals and mid-career education. These smaller events can be one-day events or mini-conferences that are hosted by a partnership between professional organizations.

There are also conferences hosted by allied trades or groups in related fields which can offer value. Many suppliers, such as malt or hop producers, hold their own conferences and seminars, as do distribution and wholesale partners. Allied industries from the alcoholic beverage sector such as distilling, wine, and cider hold their own seminars, and while the context of the

---

2   Not only could CBC seminars be held in just a literal handful of rooms during the earliest editions, but the entire conference attendance could be housed on a single hotel floor.
3   Dori Whitney, "Salute to MBAA — 100 Years," *Brewers Digest*, August 1987, 16.

material may be different, there is overlap between operations. Fundamentally, it comes down to what problems you are trying to solve. Sometimes finding out just how much you don't know about a topic can go a long way toward framing next steps.

Thinking a bit further outside the box, there is value to be gained from other sectors, whether it is organic or local agriculture groups or restaurant trade associations. While large conferences often hold individual seminars on topics such as social media management, employment law, or consumer trends, attending dedicated conferences or events that are centered around those topics will yield a deeper awareness than a single hour-long presentation.

Advanced Training Opportunities

Conferences, by their nature, offer a series of short talks across a broad range of topics. A tasting flight, if you will. These short-form pieces work well at getting a general overview of a topic or learning new approaches to a challenge, but for in-depth instruction you need to invest more dedicated time to a specific topic. These opportunities can come in a variety of forms. Extended seminars or short-term courses offer a reasonably high value-to-time commitment ratio, while more traditional academic coursework or technical training programs arm attendees with a deeper set of skills.

The brewing industry has developed a wide variety of short-term courses and opportunities. Conferences frequently offer day-long pre-conference programs on specific topics that deliver a much deeper dive than the regular conference material. The Brewers Association holds a series of day-long quality seminars throughout the year, while several equipment manufacturers and industry suppliers host dedicated multiday programs in their areas of expertise. Prime examples of such on-site training include the Ball Canning School, the Micromatic Draught Program, and the annual extravaganza known as hop selection in Yakima.

There are also numerous programs that offer a blend of practical and theoretical knowledge. There are annual courses offered by the MBAA as well as the ASBC, while more traditional institutions such as UC-Davis and the Siebel Institute have courses designed to offer continuing education opportunities

on topics ranging from brewing microbiology to sensory evaluation to engineering. These courses traditionally have been built around one- to two-week curricula and taught on-site, but many of these programs are going virtual and being presented through online formats.

Casting the net even wider, there are a wide variety of learning opportunities that aren't specific to brewing but directly pertain to your operations. Some of these are regulatory driven: 10- and 30-hour courses offered by OSHA are particularly relevant, while breweries that expand into non-alcoholic product lines are required to have at least one person certified as a Preventive Control Qualified Individual (PCQI) through an accredited program (Pellettieri and Nicholas 2020).

Keeping Training In-House

Expertise comes at a price, so bringing some of these skill sets in-house can yield dividends. For example, train-the-trainer courses can qualify employees to certify others on alcoholic beverage service programs such as Training for Intervention ProcedureS (TIPS), as well as skills such as forklift operations and CPR and first aid. Costs for hiring third parties to teach these courses can quickly rack up, even more so when refresher training and certification is needed. Having one or more employees qualified to lead these courses has a direct benefit internally, and they can also be a resource for the wider community.

Training expenses are investments that pay off over time, but the costs are still real in the immediate term and can pose a barrier to making that investment. One way to potentially defray costs is to look for grants from state and local governments. Grant programs from a state department of labor for locally sponsored discounts to training sessions can go a long way toward making an opportunity affordable.[4] Be warned, there is a great deal of variation between different state agency offices. Some state agencies offer programs that provide matching grants for any form of safety expenditure, while others offer apprenticeship programs and grant funding specific to training, so you will have to do some digging to find what is available to you in your state. It can be worth it though, so persevere with your online sleuthing. You might start by using search terms like *OSHA*, *department of labor*, *apprenticeship*,

4   For an example of one individual's journey through such a program, see Eisha Misra, "Beer and Apprenticeship: A Q&A session with Samantha Fox," U.S. Department of Labor Blog, June 14, 2021, https://blog.dol.gov/2021/06/14/beer-and-apprenticeship-a-qa-session-with-samantha-powers.

grant, and *brewery* in various combinations and see what programs turn up in your state.

Acquiring and upgrading computer skills is equally relevant to brewery operations: not everything in the brewery involves stainless steel. Developing deeper expertise in accounting software packages and enterprise resource planning (ERP) programs can reduce consultant costs derived from troubleshooting and other projects, if not avoid them entirely. Even having a better understanding of the full range of features in common spreadsheet packages and other workplace software will add value. Most of us barely scratch the surface of the capabilities built into modern workplace software tools. Accessing these capabilities can dramatically increase the usefulness of existing software, but this takes training to accomplish.

Just to use the spreadsheet example, knowing how to develop pivot tables, build Gantt charts, use statistical formulae correctly, or nest calculations across multiple tabs will have applications across the entire organization, from accounting to retail to brewing to sales. Looking at more niche software such as project management or maintenance tracking tools can unlock even more value. Some employees will have this experience from previous employment or will develop it out of their own curiosity, but you should not depend on that. Spending money to actively develop these skills within your team will see a tremendous return on investment.

Collaborations and Field Trips

Collaborations and field trips aren't always viewed as professional development, but the potential is there. As with a conference, one of the advantages of collaborations is networking with other professionals. These relationships allow you to troubleshoot by asking questions at a peer-to-peer level, but "collabs" have other benefits. Just actively observing how other breweries are organized can offer lessons you can apply at home, so collaborations are a learning opportunity if you take a deliberate approach.

Field trips to suppliers or even other brewery taprooms are useful experiences from a morale and team-building standpoint, but they can also be approached from the professional development angle. Seeing how others approach common problems is always valuable—field trips can be a source for clever ideas, new insights, or even just having a better understanding of why your brewery is structured the way that it is.

LEVERAGING HIGHER EDUCATION

Avenues to gain job-related skills can come through a variety of programs, but community colleges are an excellent and often overlooked resource. While large research universities draw most of the attention, community colleges are hidden jewels within the educational system, offering a particular focus on skills training for the local job market and continuing education for adults throughout their careers. Short courses for job-related skills are the bread and butter of community colleges and central to their mission. Additionally, they are built around adapting to the schedules of working people, not just the traditional full-time student. Programs built around brewery-focused curricula are increasingly common.

Longer-form training is also available through many community colleges or their four-year cousins, and these opportunities also have significant value in the brewery. Learning to code the ladder logic used by a programmable logic controller (PLC) is a prime example. Ladder logic is embedded in almost every piece of automated equipment, and while complex sequences may still require an outside contractor, having staff members able to perform minor adjustments to equipment timing or sensor activity is incredibly useful.

Skills such as basic welding or plumbing fall into a similar category. Exploring training programs at vocational training centers offers enormous benefits. Being able to quickly repair a broken bracket or tap into a water line for a simple faucet will help preserve cashflow for more significant projects that require the involvement of more highly skilled tradespeople.

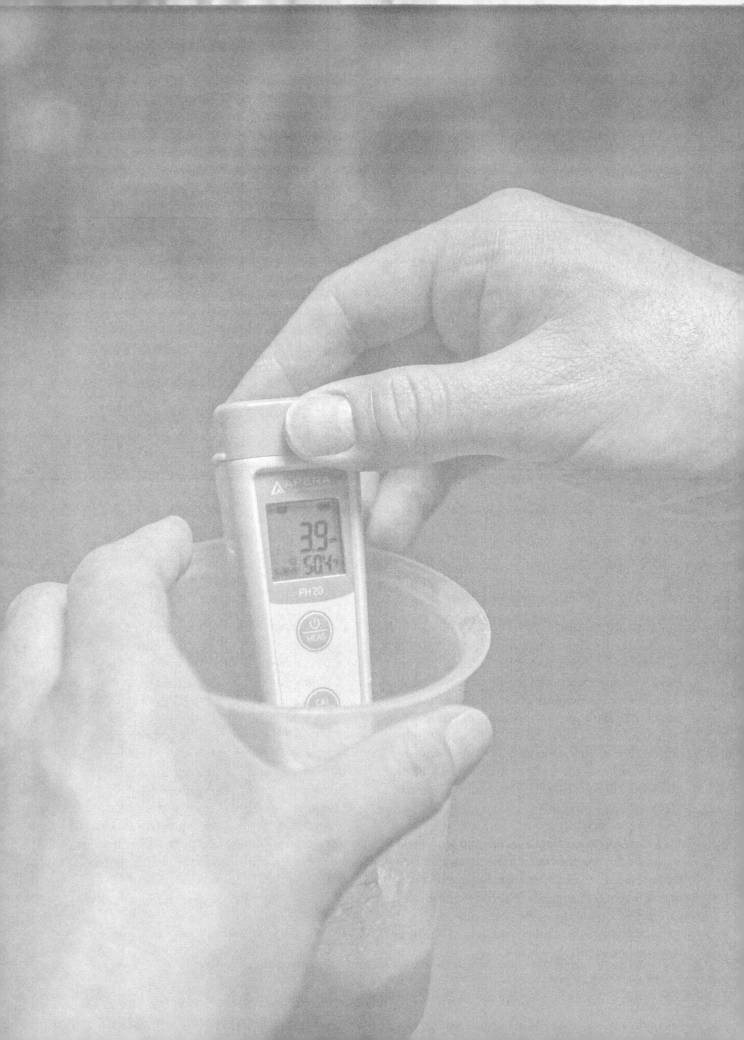

PERFORMANCE ASSESSMENTS

Every single workday, your staff members are establishing a record of how they approach and perform their roles. The question is, are you paying attention and, importantly, reacting appropriately to that record? Performance reviews are often dreaded by both employees and managers alike. Done poorly, they are generic, sometimes outright anonymous, and don't offer any useable information to either party.

This is a tragedy, because recognizing the way that people perform their roles is essential to having a successful and resilient organizational culture. Honest feedback is crucial to growth, both for an individual and the larger team. Telling a colleague that they are doing fine because you want to avoid a difficult conversation takes away their opportunity to adjust. This avoidance is also noticed by others, either directly or inferred. Seeing poor performance persist day after day takes a toll on the other team members who are picking up the slack. The reverse is also true: when success is treated with a shrug, it can cut off motivation at the knees. Both scenarios can lead staff to look for other opportunities. Skilled employees will always have options, especially in vibrant job markets.

Providing open and honest feedback helps the brewery consistently meet expectations, set attainable and relevant goals, and maintain a pathway for communication across the company. Communication needs to go both ways to be effective: a performance assessment done well is not a one-way street. When employees don't feel like they have a voice, the risk is that they'll stop using it. It's important to give people space to ask for clarity or guidance. Just because you think you made instructions or expectations clear doesn't mean you did. When employees become reluctant to ask questions or seek guidance, the potential for errors and conflicts increases significantly.

People need to be allowed to express concerns and grievances in the workplace. It's tempting to avoid hearing complaints, but that comes down to framing. An everyday definition of "complaint" boils down to "feedback we don't want to hear." No matter how frustrating or painful, some concerns are real and need to be heard and acknowledged. Employee reports about problems happening in the brewery need to be addressed, even if the delivery isn't particularly artful.

You also need to acknowledge that assessments are easily biased, consciously or not. An all-too-common example in the brewing industry involves discounting the opinion or experience of women in the field. Also common is assigning more importance to job titles than actual work history, such as valuing opinions based on a stint in the brewhouse over a record of achievement in packaging or another industry.

The immediate bias categories that come to mind are preconceptions around race, age, gender, or sexual identity; however, bias can extend beyond those into assumptions about areas such as educational background, parental status, or military service. Even when these biases don't constitute overt harassment, they can influence the content and delivery of feedback, as well as how professional development opportunities are distributed.

Throughout this chapter, there will be a focus on selecting and applying metrics that are based on specific, relevant criteria and that can be communicated in a clear and equitable way.

COMMON FLAWS WITH PERFORMANCE ASSESSMENTS

- Personal opinions masquerading as objective assessments
- Ratings categories that don't reflect actual work priorities
- Scoring metrics that aren't connected to specific behaviors and actions
- The temptation to "protect people"

PERFORMANCE AND FALSE EQUIVALENCIES

Before we dive into approaches for performance assessments, it is important to make it clear what they are versus what they are not. Regardless of whether you call them assessments, evaluations, or reviews, the purpose of the assessment process is to maximize potential, whether that is individual, team-based, or across the entire organization. Effective performance assessments involve teams as much as they do individuals. There are two fundamental misunderstandings that both employees and companies frequently make during this process.

First, evaluating performance isn't the same thing as taking disciplinary action. This mindset generally comes from allowing issues to build to a breaking point, but the two are genuinely separate. Assessments need to be attuned to the full range of performance, both good and bad. If the only time you talk about performance is when there is a problem, operators are going to retreat into a defensive stance rather than being open to feedback. When there are performance issues that trigger a disciplinary process, that process is separate and apart from evaluation. An assessment should be neutral and

describe how performance relates to a set of expectations. Discipline looks at what gets done about a specific incident or trend. They are separate tracks.

Similarly, performance and compensation may be linked, but they definitely aren't equivalent and should not be conflated. Yes, breweries are businesses with budgets, and the size of the compensation budget is affected by the financial performance of the business. But while there is obviously a link between operational performance and financial performance, this relationship isn't directly linear. It's hard to maintain healthy finances for long when there is poor performance, but superlative performance doesn't immediately result in a strong balance sheet. There are simply too many other factors involved. Good performance absolutely should be recognized and compensated, but performance and pay rates aren't always going to be the same conversation.

Having a formal performance assessment policy is a useful tool for documenting how this process is organized, which encourages accountability and provides a reference point for checking whether managers are applying criteria consistently. Components should include a basic schedule of when assessments are conducted, the metrics used to rate performance, and how merit pay raises are granted. How this latter point is applied will vary from brewery to brewery, but common factors include hitting performance targets or individual and team objectives. This pays dividends when looking over payroll as part of an annual budget review.

REAL-TIME PERFORMANCE ASSESSMENTS

Not every review needs to cover an entire year or quarter. Regular, frequent interactions can catch performance issues early and correct behavior before they become trends or result in significant incidents. There are additional benefits. Actively and consistently engaging with people builds trust. Without that, it's difficult to share concerns about technical processes or interactions with other staff. Confiding incidents of harassment or abuse is difficult enough; sharing painful information with someone you don't trust is essentially a non-starter. The same holds true for employees struggling with substance abuse or other personal crises.

Maintaining communication depends on trust and isn't a passive process. There are several ways to approach this process ranging from purely informal conversations to loosely structured meetings. These

DISCUSSING PERFORMANCE AND COMPENSATION

Discussions around compensation tend to happen at very specific intervals: when employees are initially hired, when an employee requests a raise, and during performance evaluations. That initial conversation will be driven by two factors, namely the position's listed wage range and the skills and experience the new hire will bring to the role. This is an estimate of *value*: a highly skilled hire brings more to the table than someone who needs to be trained from the ground up, so pay should be commensurate with that value.

It is important to recognize that this starts as an estimate. Once an employee has had the opportunity to demonstrate their value, how payroll budgets are distributed can and should change. A common approach is to schedule a review at the end of the employee's orientation and training cycle, whether that is on 30, 60, or 90 days. As an employee's skills increase, the added value they bring deserves an increase in pay.

When an employee approaches management and asks for a raise, the first step should be to schedule a time to review their performance. The key metric here is value: how are they improving the brewery? Performance reviews will inform this assessment. A demonstrated history of taking on projects and delivering improvements (or not) goes a long way toward making a case. The response may be an immediate pay increase or the discussion can lay out a pathway that will lead to a raise, whether that involves taking on additional responsibilities or another form of professional development. This pathway should never be a barrier: the goal is to work together to increase value.

Annual reviews are the traditional venue for discussing pay raises. Ideally, owners and management should have made time to assess the financial health of the brewery and lay out a payroll budget for the next fiscal year. Either way, putting in the effort to have genuine performance reviews will establish a fact-based record for employees and managers to work from. The key factor here is to give consistent, regular feedback throughout the year, regardless of when compensation decisions are made. Leaving it to a single touchpoint each year doesn't provide an adequate opportunity to establish an accurate record of an employee's value or their potential.

THE "WE'RE A FAMILY…" CANARD

There is a phrase that pops up among small businesses that goes something like, "We pride ourselves on being like a family." Many small businesses are family-owned, and breweries are no exception. Even when the founders are a group of close friends, there is a clear connection. The identification is understandable: after all, breweries are small, like-minded groups of people who spend enormous amounts of time together, *ergo* a family. That said, it's a strange formulation. As a rule, families don't issue biweekly paychecks to their members or carry workers' compensation insurance. This construction of brewery-as-family sounds like a positive attribute, but it is a deeply flawed view of how an organization functions.

The problem is that the family concept is vulnerable to becoming a mask for arbitrary rules and compliance. Breweries can and should have a common set of values, standards, and motivations, but that is not the same as imposing viewpoints onto employees that have nothing to do with the workplace. A lot of disruptive, if not outright toxic, behavior can be waved away by "but we're a family," but that doesn't make it any better. The power dynamics and structures of a family simply are not the same as a business.

techniques may not appear to be performance assessments in the strictest sense, but they serve an important function in recognizing and addressing behaviors in real time. The scale of the organization can be a factor here, but the importance of building and maintaining trust is a constant. In a brewery with a small staff, everyone works together regularly, from the top tier of management to the newest part-time hire. This doesn't mean that everything is hunky-dory and folks all get along, but personal-professional connections are easy to establish and maintain. A larger brewery has to put in more effort to develop the same level of engagement across the organization, especially when remote staff or multiple locations are involved.

Personal Check-Ins

These are an incredibly useful practice with employees. Personal check-ins can be informal, such as simply asking people how their day is going and how you could help, or something more structured like a monthly one-on-one about workplace matters. Regardless of format, the goal for these check-ins is to maintain open lines of communication. This isn't about being friends with everyone: it's about not being detached from the daily realities of your team. When problems need to be discussed, having a common pool of understanding matters. This is true whether it is a manager pointing out a performance issue or employees bringing up a problem. For a message to be heard effectively, there needs to be mutual respect.

Pre-Shift Meetings

Bringing a team together prior to starting a shift is a valuable practice that borders on essential. Pre-shift meetings, or huddles, provide a forum for communicating the day's goals and priorities, sharing updates on schedules or menus, and ensuring that everyone is on the same page and has an opportunity to ask questions to clarify any points of confusion. Issues from previous shifts should be raised here, along with any resolutions that have happened.

Another feature to these sessions is the chance to live up to the adage "praise in public, punish in private." Pre-shift meetings offer a way to highlight employees' successes to the entire group, while also allowing problems to be discussed at a team-level, rather than focusing on an individual. A workplace is a communal organism: addressing problems at

DOCUMENTING INTERACTIONS

Small, close-knit teams often appear as though everyone is on the same page by virtue of their constant communication. The problem here is that memories are faulty, and just because you all work closely together, that doesn't mean that everything is automatically shared across the team. It's easy to assume that everyone knows a key piece of information when that isn't actually the case. As the size and number of teams increases, this challenge is exacerbated. Documenting important information is critical for accountability.

On the operations side, personal check-ins generally don't need to be documented: they are casual by design. However, when leaders learn about a significant piece of information that merits a follow-up, writing it down helps to ensure that it doesn't slip through the cracks. Having a small notebook handy to capture information throughout the day or week is an important tool. The same idea extends into pre-shift huddles and other team meetings.

For situations that involve problems around respect or unprofessional behavior, documentation takes on more importance. Effective investigations are particularly dependent on documentation, so having written, dated notes is essential. As organizations grow, choosing an appropriate implementation for documenting manager-employee interactions will always be a tricky balancing act. Breweries may need to transition from one model of HR documentation/record-keeping to another, and management should be aware of that. Addressing this in advance is far better than trying to adapt in the middle of a crisis, particularly for the affected employees.

the individual level is necessary, but long-term success will depend on group dynamics. Reinforcing the behavior you want and consistently setting expectations with the team on a clear and consistent basis is the key to successful execution.

These huddles don't need to take much time. Absent significant issues, they will rarely take much more than five or ten minutes. This is time well spent, even if circumstances require taking double or triple that amount of time. Just like athletes stretch their muscles prior to working out, spending time upfront to prepare the team before their day begins is more efficient than information coming out late or not at all.

A simple best practice is to write these notes on a whiteboard. This helps staff members check against their own memory throughout the day. Typing up these pre-shift notes is useful but can be a burden. A simple way to document them over time is to take a photo of the notes, whether they are on paper or the whiteboard. Uploading a photo is often easier for small breweries that have limited numbers of computers available to front-line teams. For breweries that use platforms such as Slack, notes can be uploaded and shared across multiple teams.

Figure 4.1 offers a template for pre-shift huddles for several production-side teams, but this kind of meeting will work for any functional group within the brewery. A typical pre-shift huddle might address the following topics:

- Safety concerns
- Quality concerns
- Maintenance
- Menu and news
- Scheduling
- Q&A

Groups who operate in shifts, such as opening and closing shift brewers, may have more of a hand-off than a huddle, but the basic structure still applies. The goal is to share critical, relevant information, something leadership should ensure happens.

Pre-Shift Meeting Agenda Examples

Daily Production Pre-Shift
- Safety concerns—current conditions and updates
  - Summer heat warnings: Describe signs of heat-induced distress, emphasize hydration, and add breaks
  - Recent injury from chemical exposure: Deliver refresher on PPE and handling corrosive compounds
- Quality concerns—current areas of focus
  - Glycol valve on FV03 stuck in the open position yesterday and prematurely crashed the tank—talk through next steps
- Maintenance—updates on what's working and what isn't
  - Working on repairing the glycol solenoid on FV03
  - Boiler needs to be blown down daily—don't skip this step
- Scheduling—the day's goals, priorities, and timelines
- Q&A / Comments

Taproom Opening Pre-Shift
- Safety concerns—current conditions, documented violations, and updates
  - Fire exits were obstructed: keep them clear
- Quality concerns—current areas of focus
  - Increased fruit fly activity around taps—step up cleaning
- Maintenance— updates what's working and what isn't
  - No issues reported: confirm with group
- Menu and news—updates on the beer list, special events, review recent managers log, etc.
  - New beer coming on today: Taste and go over sell sheet
  - Scheduled to be a stop on an organized pub crawl tonight: be prepared for a rush, watch for over-served guests
- Scheduling—the day's goals, priorities, and timelines
- Q&A / Comments
  - Need to order more credit card receipt paper—almost out

Figure 4.1. Having an agenda goes a long way toward making the pre-shift huddle a productive experience for staff.

Team Meetings

Holding periodic meetings is a good technique for keeping teams on track. The frequency will vary depending on circumstances, but weekly or biweekly (i.e., every two weeks) team meetings are effective for groups that deal with rapidly changing information or complex coordination. Frequency is especially important when the team members work remotely. Without daily contact, hosting a relatively frequent call or meeting can keep each team member on the same page and allow them to receive feedback from the group.

Groups who work together on a regular basis still need a forum where members can communicate as a group. This may be at the department level for teams who are spread across shifts or workdays, such as shift brewers or taproom staff. Team meetings can be as much about recognizing accomplishments and keeping the team apprised of upcoming plans as they are about addressing problematic behavior or missed expectations. When conducted monthly or even quarterly, they become built-in opportunities for safety refresher sessions and other forms of professional development.

SCHEDULED ASSESSMENTS

The most common forms of performance assessments are annual reviews, closely followed by ones scheduled after an orientation period, such as 60- or 90-day reviews. For many employees, these are the only organized assessments they experience. The real-time assessments we've discussed up to now are geared toward identifying issues early and reacting to them. However, there is considerable value in looking back over a body of work extending across a longer period of time. Taking a longer view provides a better assessment of an employee's overall performance by separating it from the hurly-burly of daily operations.

Capturing the Full Picture

A common flaw with performance reviews is that they often don't accurately reflect the entire review period. Managers frequently don't take notes throughout the year, so the review may only be representative of the past few weeks rather than 90 days, much less a full year. This is a disservice to everyone involved.

Making a point of jotting down notes on performance, both good and bad, for each employee is essential to generating a fair picture of their performance. These don't need to be lengthy: just capturing highlights and lowlights as they occur will help. The practice of regular check-ins will serve to establish a baseline, but longer-term notes help to document significant moments in time that could easily be forgotten later down the line. Acknowledging and recording highlights is particularly important. As anyone who has read through online reviews can attest, negative incidents tend to linger in the memory more than the positive episodes. Making sure that you detail a full picture across the review period is essential to a fair assessment.

There are specialized HR and performance assessment software packages on the market, but simpler, low-cost options exist. Many computer operating systems have native note-taking apps where information can be quickly jotted down, while cloud-based services such as Google or the Apple ecosystems have their own tools. Having a different note tab for each employee helps to keep information organized and allows tagging entries with labels, allowing for searchability and tracking. The time-honored paper notebook also works. However this information is tracked, maintaining confidentiality is essential. Notebooks that get left in a restroom or note-taking apps left open and visible on a computer screen are an effective way to dissolve employees' trust. The trick for making any of these formats work is taking the time to jot down those notes and compile a record of performance.

Gathering Information

Direct observation isn't always the best method for collecting information: breweries have a lot going on, and the reality is that you simply aren't going to notice everything that happens in the brewery. Additional sources of information you can use include reviews of primary sources, such as brew sheets and other process logs, taproom logs, timecards, and sales platforms. These sources can help differentiate between an isolated incident and a legitimate trend. A single incident may be significant enough to warrant action, but generally looking for trends will provide a better picture of performance.

Another valuable tool that bridges the gap between real-time assessments and longer-term reviews is the weekly recap. Building out a detailed weekly review of activity provides a valuable record of events over time. Having these records is useful in a variety of ways, starting with being able to look back at your own recaps to provide context and recall. Tasking leaders with generating recaps for their respective areas or departments helps to create a more complete overview for senior leaders or ownership. In addition to being a valuable tool for leadership, weekly recaps provide a contemporaneous record for individuals to bolster their own case during a review later down the line.

Deciding What to Measure

There is a saying that directly pertains to performance assessments: you can't manage what you don't measure. This is true, but it lacks some critical context. You also have to know *what* you want to manage and which metrics will provide useful information in this regard before you begin assessing people.

Fortunately, you should already have something in your brewery that starts to address these issues: the job description, which we looked at in chapter 1. If the job description accurately articulates what the brewery expects from a specific position, it will also reflect what is expected from the employee: is the employee performing each task effectively or not? The job description's list of duties provides a common frame of reference for both the reviewer and the employee. As a bonus, because job descriptions are specific to each role, you will be comparing apples to apples rather than forcing a one-size-fits-all review format.

Job descriptions are an excellent starting point, but there are significant advantages to building evaluation formats that are specifically tailored to brewery priorities. Tables 4.1 and 4.2 give examples of how evaluation categories can be applied to different positions in a department.

When we compare tables 4.1 and 4.2, a few things jump out. First, there are similarities to the more generic templates you may have seen. This is going to be unavoidable to a degree. The difference here is that the category selections are deliberately chosen and worded. The core competencies of a shift brewer and packaging manager will be different, just as their job descriptions will be. A common misconception is that becoming a manager is the natural next step for a skilled operator. There's nothing natural about it: managerial skills are a category all on their own. An assessment form needs to reflect that the metrics for that role involve facilitating team success through communication and planning more than mastery of the tri-clamp or beer pouring skills. Generic forms will fall short on these distinctions.

THE PROBLEM WITH GENERIC TEMPLATES

However you decide to gather and store information, a critical step involves deciding which factors to track. Breweries are filled to overflowing with data that you can track, and performance data are no different. The purpose of performance assessments is to maximize and unlock the potential across individuals, teams, and the whole brewery. Creating good data from these assessments requires an understanding of what contributes to the brewery's performance and culture.

A cursory internet search for annual review templates will reveal a variety of examples. Common features are fields such as *quality of work, punctuality and attendance, communication skills*, and *decision-making*. Rating scales may be numeric or offer various statements on how well employees meet expectations. As a rule, these are generic to the point of being arbitrary and useless. There are several flaws with these formats, but we'll focus on two.

Metrics that don't match the brewery's core values: Most review forms have fields that are important in theory but are stated so broadly that they're difficult to apply consistently. It's also challenging to apply the same review form to employees with significantly different roles and job functions. Punctuality and attendance will have very different meanings when applied to a graphic designer versus a brewer or bartender.

Undefined scales: On a 0–9 scale, what is the objective difference between a score of 7 versus 8 for *communication skills*? Are the specific expectations for decision-making documented somewhere, and would all managers arrive at the same evaluation score? This doesn't mean that communication isn't important, because it is, but employees need to understand what a rating means if they're expected to improve their score.

Table 4.1 **Evaluation Categories: Production leadership**

Safety	Committed to promoting safety rules and practices; eliminates safety hazards when identified; leads by example
Leadership	Use of positive and proactive leadership to develop staff and promote company strategies and values
Communication, Interpersonal skills	Ability to communicate with others clearly and effectively
Teamwork	Ability to work with others in a collaborative manner; can lead effective teams who deliver value-added outcomes by working together
Job knowledge, Technical skills	Knowledge of departmental processes, relevant industry practices, and company operations
Productivity, Efficiency, Quality	Completion of high-quality work in a timely manner; wisely uses time to complete necessary job duties
Initiative, Innovation	Takes the initiative to develop innovative systems and processes
Housekeeping, Organization	Leads and promotes good housekeeping principles and system organization

Table 4.2 **Evaluation Categories: Production operator**

Safety	Commitment to safe work practices, the elimination of safety hazards, and use of personal protective equipment
Interpersonal skills	Ability to work alone or with others in a team environment; communicates effectively with their own and other departments; accepts constructive criticism and conducts themself professionally
Quality	Works effectively to produce the necessary quality product
Environmental and sanitation knowledge	Awareness of sanitation and environmental requirements; maintains and applies good housekeeping principles
Job knowledge, Productivity	Knowledge of departmental processes/procedures and equipment operation; ability to work efficiently
Initiative	Willingness to accept responsibility for actions and willingness to take action when necessary; ability to work independently

Having said that, there is considerable overlap between the two sets of evaluation criteria. Again, this is a deliberate act. Safety leads off both lists because safety is foundational to everything we do in the brewery. Beyond that, the lists are tailored to the requirements of the individual roles, both in terms of the categories themselves and the specifics of the short descriptive text that follows them. The category list for taproom staff and sales representatives will have even more differences; for example, it will have an "Interpersonal Skills—Customer Service" category.

Building a form that is specific to your brewery helps focus the mind and direct the effort that goes into evaluations. One of the reasons that people dread reviews is that they can feel completely divorced from what is really happening in the brewery. Evaluating staff on the same set of priorities you discussed during the orientation phase (chap. 2) is a message in and of itself and helps to keep the process relevant.

The objective is to create a set of evaluation forms that reflect the brewery and its goals. Your application of this approach will likely be heavily modified to fit your workplace. It may even be entirely different in tone and approach. Whatever you choose, the point of this exercise is to be deliberate about your choices on how to assess performance and deliver feedback.

Presenting Performance
So That It Is Understood

Regardless of whether we use the job description or a custom form, the next step involves developing a rating system that goes beyond arbitrary scores. As noted earlier, numeric scoring systems struggle with differentiating between scores in a meaningful way. Numeric scores are intended to represent a particular value, but the number itself doesn't contain that information. Unless you define what a 7 represents, people are going to bring their own meaning to the table. The difference between 7 and 8 is mathematically clear, but to an employee it comes across more as random. This is true for reviewers as well, to be honest.

Expectation-based systems have their own issues. They're basically numeric scales in disguise, although there is the advantage that they at least start to assign a meaning to the numbers. Ratings based on five-point continuums that range from, for example, "Poor" to "Outstanding" or "Below Expectations" to "Regularly Exceeds Expectations" seem reasonably clear, but unless the actual expectations are clearly laid out, they are still largely open to interpretation. Employees may have very different pictures of what constitutes "above average" across a team, especially if real-time assessments haven't been consistently in practice throughout the review period.

Another pair of common review formats are the paragraph and conversational assessments. Both are ways to avoid using a scale, and they offer the opportunity for more nuance than "exceeds expectations." Where they struggle is that they can slip into a free-form trap. Conversational assessments can be breezy and quick, or they can end up being contentious back-and-forth exchanges. Either way, they don't leave a comprehensive record, so the parties involved can leave the session with dramatically different ideas and memories of what was said or decided. A month or a year later, this lack of commonality can become a problem. Paragraph evaluations have a different set of challenges. There is no shortage of a record, but generating written reviews for a team of ten rapidly becomes a slog. Trying to describe a year's worth of effort for the whole group tends to end up with constantly recycling language.

Descriptive Assessments

Descriptive assessments can help square the circle. Rather than a rating scale that runs from "Unacceptable"

to "Excellent," which are open to interpretation and dispute, a descriptive format creates a series of ratings that clearly lay out a set of behaviors that describe performance. These are still interpretive, but they indicate performance in a way that is not so open-ended. The overall goal is to have a common framework that allows employees to see themselves in a specific score and understand why they aren't rated differently. Traditional review formats are skewed toward management because they're one-way devices, but descriptive assessments offer advantages for both parties during a review.

By clearly defining each rating score, everyone can make an evidence-based case for a score. This is another area where maintaining a set of weekly recaps can pay dividends: they're a contemporaneous record and provide performance information across the entire review period. Well-written descriptions of each score should allow people to recognize the parameters of each rating and see themselves within that score. Additionally, that level of detail offers employees a chance to point out behaviors and events from the review period that provide evidence for a different score. It's hard to argue for an "8" over a "7," but allowing an employee to describe how their body of work fits better into one category over another gives them an opportunity for persuasion and evidence.

DELIVERING ASSESSMENTS

How a message is communicated is as important as the message itself, if not more so. With the real-time assessments, the key was providing space for two-way communication. Structured formal assessments are no different. Acknowledging the humanity of employees is an important part of the process. It is particularly significant with respect to recognizing and supporting mental health and wellness. Compensation is a motivator, but feeling respected, engaged, and supported in the workplace is typically a larger factor in retention and performance.

Self-Ratings

Looking at tables 4.3 and 4.4, note that both have a column for self-rating. Allowing an employee to get a copy of the review form and rate themselves before sitting down with their manager has significant advantages. First, self-ratings call for people to take an active role in the assessment process. Second, the ability to see the scoring criteria in advance demystifies how

Table 4.3 **Scoring Example: Brewery-wide safety expectations**

Safety: Commitment to safe work practices, the elimination of safety hazards, and use of personal protective equipment		
Self Rating	**Supervisor Rating**	**Select one of the behavioral categories below.**
☐	☐	Not concerned with safety; causes or allows unsafe conditions to exist. May have a history of incidents as a result of unsafe practices.
☐	☐	Understands the basics of safety but may ignore safe working practices in favor of getting tasks done faster or more easily.
☐	☐	Has acceptable knowledge of safety requirements, routinely follows safe working practices, and completes required safety training. Correctly wears required PPE, including eye and ear protection.
☐	☐	Observes and promotes safety rules. Proactively resolves potential safety concerns within area of responsibility. Demonstrates excellent safety awareness.
☐	☐	Actively focuses on good safety principles. Promotes safety, suggests improvements, and helps to resolve safety concerns whenever observed.
Courtesy of Bell's Brewery, Inc.		

Table 4.4 **Scoring Example: Communication skills for a production leader**

Communications—Interpersonal Skills: Ability to communicate with others clearly and effectively		
Self Rating	**Supervisor Rating**	**Select one of the behavioral categories below**
☐	☐	Not able to communicate effectively. Creates occasional misunderstandings and may alienate others.
☐	☐	Communications may sometimes be unclear, incomplete, one directional, or short in nature. May not encourage interactive discussions.
☐	☐	Provides clear direction to employees even when the message is difficult or unpopular. Communicates with and listens effectively to employee issues and needs. Portrays a service-oriented mindset with all staff by being approachable.
☐	☐	Communicates information frequently and ensures that employees understand the big picture for the area in a timely manner. Actively utilizes two-way communications to ensure conversations with employees are open and effective.
☐	☐	Uses multiple communication methods to ensure that information is clearly understood. Consistently asks for feedback to ensure that communications are effective. Recognized as a leader in effective communications and assists teammates to do the same.
Courtesy of Bell's Brewery, Inc.		

performance is being measured. The categories themselves are a statement of priorities, and the employee can then begin thinking about how they fit within the rating system. This provides a chance to think through events from the review period and build their best case for each category. Arriving to a review session without having had this opportunity forces the employee to think on the fly, creating a structural disadvantage.

If maximizing potential is the goal, ambushing your employees won't help.

Discussion

Providing time and space to go through the ratings with an employee is important. Ideally, robust real-time assessments will lead to the formal scores from the employee and manager being the same.

Realistically, there are going to be occasional differences. Talking through those differences and giving examples is an important facet of the assessment process. If you're not prepared to explain decisions and provide examples, the process slips back to appearing arbitrary.

You can include areas for comments on the assessment forms. These provide a way to give more detail about specific areas, memorialize key points from the discussion, or, if necessary, document any disagreements over a rating. Again, the overall goal is to work from a common frame of reference. Documentation limits how far stories can drift over time.

Comfort levels with verbal, real-time discussions vary from person to person—not everyone is a natural at speaking on the fly about their performance or difficult topics. Offering a list of discussion points helps to prime the pump during the session and allows people more comfortable with written formats a chance to prepare their own notes so they can fully express themselves during the meeting. Finding out what people most enjoy, where they struggle, and how they can be supported goes a long way toward helping employees stay engaged.

Sample Discussion Points
1. How do you feel the last year has been for you professionally, and why?
2. What do you consider to be your most important achievements in the past year?
3. What goals are in still in progress that haven't been completed to date?
4. What can I do to better support you in your work?
5. What aspects of your job do you find most rewarding? Which are the most frustrating or difficult?
6. Are you doing anything that doesn't seem to add value? How can we change or eliminate that?
7. What do you see as our most important tasks and goals for the next year?
8. Where would you like to focus over the next year? How can we support that?

The discussion phase is also an opportunity for other issues to be raised. In some cases, these will involve interpersonal matters, some minor, others not. These may not be comfortable to hear but ignoring underlying problems won't solve them. Staff accountability is central to successful long-term operations, regardless of roles within the organization.

Goals

Discussions are also a platform to talk through and establish goals. Reviewing plans from previous sessions informs the assessment of the current period, while laying down new goals helps to provide a roadmap for the coming year. Achievability is critical: there has to be a realistic path to success.

Goals may be assigned after discussion. These may be oriented toward a technical challenge facing the wider team or toward individual efforts, such as being the point person on a major equipment purchase and installation or calling on a certain number of accounts per month.

Other goals may be aimed directly at professional growth. Examples include qualifying as a full operator on additional equipment or cross-training in a new area, submitting a presentation proposal or poster to a professional conference, earning an industry-related certification, or becoming the in-house subject matter expert on a particular beer style.

These goals should be leveled appropriately for the skills and experience of the employee, as the goal is to provide a road for further growth, not burnout. Setting up four to five well-defined goals is a reasonable target. It's also helpful to encourage additional personal goals that have nothing to do with the brewery. From an assessment perspective, the nature of these goals is irrelevant. Their purpose is to encourage maintaining a healthy work-life balance, again avoiding burnout.

One approach that lends structure to the goal-setting process is using the SMART goals paradigm. The advantage to this format is that it helps to provide structure when developing goals, but the focus should be on the outcomes, not the process.

SMART Goals
 S = Specific: define the task
 M = Measurable: progress be measured
 A = Achievable: the task can be completed within the time frame
 R = Relevant: the task adds value to the team
 T = Timely: the task has an appropriate level of priority

CONFRONTING PERFORMANCE ISSUES

When addressing problems, be timely, be specific, be relevant, and be consistent.

Be timely. Offering real-time feedback takes on greater urgency when there are problems occurring. Addressing issues in the moment is crucial. Allowing a negative situation to build over time until it reaches a breaking point takes away the opportunity from the employee for them to adjust their behavior. Do not put things off: if a situation is important enough to bring up in December, it was just as important when it happened back in April.

Be specific. Specificity is essential when addressing behavior. Simply telling someone that they aren't performing well is meaningless: unless you define the problem, there is no path toward making the appropriate correction. It would be like receiving sensory feedback on a new beer that just says, "Tastes bad." There's not much to go on there. Contrast that with feedback that says, "Underattenuated and astringent, with distinct creamed corn aromas behind the hop profile." That description contains considerably more information to work with. The same concept holds true for feedback on an employee's performance: people deserve to know where they need to apply themselves.

Be relevant. Following the above analogy, now imagine receiving feedback on a pilot beer that states, "I didn't like the glassware." This information is useful from a marketing and taproom service perspective, but it isn't particularly germane to dialing in a new recipe. If your feedback isn't relevant to job function and performance, take a step back and assess what you're trying to say. Feedback regarding performance needs to be relevant in order to be actionable.

Be consistent. Consistency is the glue that keeps it all together. Rules need to apply to everyone, and inconsistencies tend to be noticed. Calling out one employee for actions that are ignored in a colleague is a recipe for poor morale, not only for the affected employee but across the team as a whole. Being aware of biases and actively considering how personal opinions can influence assessments is critically important.

Clearly and consistently describing expectations for behavior in an employee manual or standalone policy is an important part of communication. Absenteeism and other performance and behavioral issues need to have well-defined standards of conduct so that every member of the team across the brewery understands what is expected of them. Individual behavior has a direct impact on the team. Getting employees to recognize this dynamic helps to develop team-oriented behavior: understanding that being unexpectedly late to work is disruptive for other team members can change perception and shift behavior from focusing on personal motivations. This awareness can't honestly be expected from employees if the expectations aren't communicated in the first place.

This also applies to positive feedback: rewarding some employees but not others for the exact same behavior has its own detrimental effects. Being seen as playing favorites is corrosive to morale and respect. To be accepted as fair, performance assessments need to be seen as consistent.

Coaching

Real-time assessments are valuable because they function as quality assurance measures. Quality assurance is all about proactive steps to lay the groundwork for successful operations in advance. (Contrast this with quality control, which involves checking events that have already happened against a set of standards.) When you engage with your teams consistently, you can stay in front of issues and catch them as they develop. If you hire and train people effectively, you will have a staff that is already motivated to perform well, so it's unlikely that someone is deliberately underperforming. Instead, your default position should be to assume that there is a disconnect between how the employee and the brewery understands expectations. Coaching employees is the opportunity to identify and bridge these gaps.

Having a clear understanding of what coaching entails is important. A professional definition of coaching would be "a deliberate process that uses focused conversations to create an environment for individual growth, purposeful action, and sustained improvement" (Ken Blanchard Companies 2020). Putting this into practice involves establishing genuine trust, identifying a set of goals, working together to develop a realistic plan of action, and then helping employees maintain accountability.

Coaching your staff may involve reviewing SOPs or reaction plans, reasserting policies and expectations, or simply listening to employees' concerns. No matter how well-developed a training program is, confidence can take time, even when the competence is already there. This also applies to experienced staff: even at the most elite levels, athletes utilize and benefit from coaches to fine-tune their craft. Taking the time to work through the mechanics or nuances of a process can make all the difference in elevating someone's performance in their role.

Investing time and effort to support employees and clarify misunderstandings early is vastly more effective than waiting. Looking the other way isn't going to solve the issue. This is particularly true when there are interpersonal conflicts. These situations are different than general performance issues. Understanding which are coachable scenarios and which may require more formal action is important to recognize. There are cases where an employee doesn't recognize how their behavior affects others. These situations can be amenable to coaching, but antagonistic and harassing behavior needs to be addressed immediately.

Performance Improvement Plans

Coaching is best suited to helping team members understand expectations and teaching them the tools of the trade. When performance issues become a function of motivation and effort rather than understanding, then coaching reaches its limits; a different approach is needed.

In these situations, you need to clearly lay out expectations and tie them to a defined time frame as well as consequences. The time frame might be 30, 60, or 90 days depending on the complexity of the goals. There are various terms and buzzwords for this concept, but we'll use the term *performance improvement plan*, or PIP. This is a deliberate choice—the purpose of these plans is to focus on performance. The goal is to establish the standard required of a team and give an individual the opportunity to meet that standard.

SEPARATIONS

In situations where an employment separation is needed, the most important task is to follow the relevant employment and labor law requirements. However, there are additional steps you can take as the employer to minimize the effect on others in the workplace.

- **Avoid surprises**
  - Employees should understand why their employment is ending.
  - Trends should be documented and communicated in real-time.
- **Prepare in advance**
  - Swift action is tempting, but without coordination it can drag out the process.
  - Have all the necessary separation paperwork ready in a packet (e.g., final paycheck, COBRA paperwork, information on transferring other benefits) so that the employee doesn't have to keep reaching out to the brewery. This also prevents harassers or otherwise abusive employees from having an excuse to return.
  - Have a plan in place for covering work requirements. This doesn't mean oversharing in advance. Rather, understand where the gaps will be and how you'll cover them.
- **Act humanely**
  - Losing a job has financial and social costs. Even when it has been a long path to that moment, it is still a significant moment.
  - Take it to a private space—separations aren't spectator sports.
  - Be clear and concise. Being professional isn't an excuse to be callous or rude.
- **Time-outs**
  - Giving people space to process events and emotions is important. Restricting separated employees from coming to the brewery taproom helps to deescalate the situation. This is true for both the separated employee, their former colleagues, and the bar staff.
  - These restrictions can be temporary or permanent, depending on circumstances.

Note that this isn't the same as progressive discipline: assessment and punishment should not be conflated. It also isn't an excuse to drive out people by setting irrelevant standards or an unachievable timeline. These performance improvement plans need to actually be *plans*. Put the time in to help get the employee back on track. They'll either step up or they won't, but they deserve the opportunity. Creating a plan with the intent of a pre-determined negative outcome is a failure of leadership.

A performance improvement plan needs to have a clear structure in order to be effective. The SMART concept is appropriate here (p. 65). The expectations placed on the employee need to be clearly defined, measurable, applicable and relevant to the problematic behavior, and have time restrictions to enforce accountability. Establishing regular check-ins on progress is one such feature. Additional features include documenting exactly what happens if the employee succeeds in improving performance, the consequences of not improving according to the set timeline, and how the progress will be recorded.

This is a topic where you should seek advice from an expert in the employment law applicable in your state. This advice may come from a qualified consultant or legal advice from an attorney who practices in this area. Such advice comes with a cost but establishing a template that complies with legal niceties is well worth the expense.

LEADERSHIP AND MANAGEMENT

Leadership and management are frequently spoken in the same breath as though they are equivalent. While it is true that one doesn't exist without the other, leadership and management are related but separate concepts and have their own roles within an organization.

Leaders, at their core, serve as inspirational examples. They are the ones seen as role models by the wider team. They can be formal leaders, such as owners, managers, and other prominent positions on an organizational chart. These people are seen as leaders by virtue of their *position*, which speaks to why it is so important they live up to the values an organization claims to cherish. People are watching and reacting accordingly.

Not every leader is in management, however. Informal leaders are found throughout a company and earn this role by virtue of their *behavior*. This is significant because leadership status doesn't always equate to being a positive role model. Employees don't need to be malicious to be negative role models: intent is less important than how the rest of the team interprets behavior and starts to justify their own. Leaders are not just those who head functional groups or teams, they can be other team members who are especially dynamic. On the positive side, their actions will serve as an example of what it means to be a good teammate, and they become the rallying force for the team during the inevitable rough patches. Unfortunately, negative voices that poison the dynamics of a group or team are also leaders in their own way.

Managers play a different core role. Yes, they are leaders, but they exist to ensure accountability. Having a robust set of training programs, social policies, and performance expectations is necessary for long-term success, but they aren't sufficient on their own. Actions govern the reality on the ground, not the plans that describe what we value.

Breweries aren't consequence-free zones: the actions you and others take on any given day will either contribute to the health of the organization or trigger financial and personal costs. Note that these consequences exist regardless of whether they're publicly acknowledged. Accountability is essentially the recognition of that dynamic and being committed to driving positive behavior. In chapter 4, we looked at performance from the individual perspective. Managers also have the task of regularly assessing the effectiveness of teams and the company overall. Managers create the structure, set the rules, and evaluate how well employees are meeting expectations. Done poorly, management becomes fixated on the rules. Effective management focuses on outcomes and makes adjustments based on results. We'll dive into that distinction later in this chapter.

Providing an effective blend of leadership and management genuinely matters. Dysfunctional organizational cultures invariably have some combination of problems coordinating these roles. The issues may reveal themselves through operational errors that result in team frustration and financial loss, but left unchecked they can become deeply structural. Power imbalances are perpetuated through biased leadership and institutionalized by poor management. Getting this right matters.

LEADERSHIP ROLES AND FUNCTIONS

To serve as an inspiration for others, the most important duties for a leader are setting the tone for their team and being a resource for their colleagues. Fundamentally, leaders exist in the minds of their peers, not the organizational chart. Their power comes from their actions, and it is important to remember that actions not taken still have an impact even if they aren't consciously noticed. During a crisis, not becoming argumentative or fixated on blame for a problem does as much to avoid negativity taking root within a team as more visible concrete steps that focus on solutions.

Leaders setting an example themselves by applying desired behaviors is essential to workplace culture: if people can't see how you define and achieve success, it becomes unnecessarily difficult for them to go about

LEADERSHIP: DEMONSTRATING CORE VALUES

If you're not willing to accept the pain real values incur, don't bother going to the trouble of formulating a values statement.

— **Patrick Lencioni,**
"Make Your Values Mean Something," *Harvard Business Review*, July 2002

Values need to be put into action in order to make a difference. Employees can distinguish between a deeply held value and an aspirational slogan. Stating that a brewery's values are "Respect, Safety, Attention to Detail" makes for a decent bumper sticker, but does not make it a reality. To be effective, these value statements need to be put into practice. This can (and probably will) be difficult, and the process will certainly take time: aspirations don't become realities overnight. But the results are worth the investment of time and effort.

Respect
- **Treat colleagues with empathy:** they're peers and partners, not puzzle pieces.
- **Call out problematic behavior:** looking the other way won't solve the issue and doesn't support the team.
- **Encourage and mentor teammates:** be the support system you would have wanted when you were in their shoes.

Safety
- **Be a safety-oriented example:** people take cues from leadership, so step up.
- **Be a vocal advocate for your teams:** your experience carries weight.
- **Take the time to teach people about hazards:** safety is a conscious choice, not something that just happens.

Attention to detail
- **Set the example with SOPs, corrective actions, and reaction plans:** if they aren't important to you, why would your teams follow them?
- **Sweat the small stuff:** quality, sustainability, and efficiency all benefit from early interventions.
- **Get rid of busywork:** every task should be connected directly to a specific purpose.
- **Listen to your team:** great ideas can come from anywhere.

doing it as part of their own roles within the organization. People thrive most when they feel supported, which is where leaders come into play. There are several factors involved in providing resources and a sense of direction. One of the more daunting aspects of leadership is that people are paying attention to what you do, but exhibiting best practices through your own work is probably the most vital part of being a leader. People reflect what they see, so positive leadership needs to present the examples you want people to follow. How do you accomplish this? Fortunately, the answer isn't "Always Be Perfect." There are more effective and realistic tools at your disposal.

Instill an Awareness of Safety, Respect, Quality, and Other Core Values

The hallmark of an effective organizational culture is one that centers attention on its people and ensures they understand what matters to the company as a whole. Mission statements have to be lived in order to become reality. Leaders have a central role in this process by providing an example to their peers and reinforcing the importance of the brewery's core values through their actions. People notice what behaviors are respected and rewarded within the organization. From a best practice standpoint, those core values should include approaches to safety, workplace respect, and quality.

Respect and dignity are essential, for the simple reason that they're central to the human experience, and morale will always be the key to unlocking an employee's potential. Emphasizing safety in the workplace is equally paramount. At best, employees who are fearful for their health and wellbeing aren't likely to be focused on their tasks. More importantly, an effective organizational culture recognizes that there is an ethical obligation to the safety and wellbeing of the employees. Quality is a topic that is discussed at length in papers and presentations, but quality isn't defined by what we say or measure. Instead, quality is defined by what we *do*. Actions and behavior matter more than policy statements and SOPs.

Your brewery's core values need to be asserted through leadership every day, not just during orientation. If you fail to establish a genuine understanding of what the brewery values, you're laying the groundwork for expensive problems later down the road. One of the more corrosive dynamics in an organization involves reprimanding an employee about something that has never been communicated as important or, worse, is inconsistently applied.

Develop a Sense of Common Purpose

Developing a sense of common purpose means that seniority and power doesn't grant someone the privilege of bypassing core values. If anything, the opposite is true: leadership has to be held to a higher standard. If you want employees to take responsibility for the work that they perform and to take pride in it, then the brewery owners and leadership have an obligation to their employees to do them same. A brewery can set expectations and communicate core values as much as it wants during orientation and training, but positive leadership has to set the example and make it clear that you're all in this together.

Make time to establish how these values are balanced within the organization. Annual or quarterly meetings can be useful from a team-building perspective, but it is the daily lived experience of the team that makes the difference. Other considerations can be factored in as well if they are important to the brewery's identity. For example, your brewery may invest in community service and engagement as a deeply held principle or lean heavily into components such as customer service, local agriculture, or sustainability. Whatever the organizational purpose may be, your employees are important enough to have the guiding tenets of the organization clearly communicated to them.

LEADERSHIP: ESTABLISHING A COMMON PURPOSE

- **Communicate clearly:** if leaders can't articulate how a brewery's vision and values connect with its real-world activities, and how employees contribute to and benefit from that vision, then there is a problem.
- **Be as transparent as reasonable:** no matter how difficult a decision may be, making it mysterious won't improve the situation.
- **Highlight the success of others:** people deserve recognition for their wins.

Deliver Consistent Messaging

Being a trusted voice starts with being trustworthy. Messages sent today need to be true tomorrow. This isn't limited to traditional communications: actions and behaviors are also messages. Effective leadership will serve as a bulwark against the hypocrisy of "do as I say, not as I do," but this requires conscious effort.

The priorities you designate as core values need to be reflected in your daily practice. If a policy or procedure can be ignored or changed on a whim, then it wasn't a core value in the first place and you shouldn't claim otherwise. Whenever you establish a priority, there needs to be a clear connection to business performance and the culture you're trying to cultivate. That connection should be communicated to employees so that they understand the "why" behind what you're trying to accomplish.

From there, it is an exercise in putting those priorities into practice. Inconsistent application eventually leads to employees making their own decisions about what is and what isn't essential, undermining the entire project. These priorities also need to apply equally across the team and wider organization. When rules apply to some but not others, it will inevitably lead to conflict. It doesn't even need to involve actual favoritism or being "above the rules": appearances become reality in the absence of other information. Explaining how rules are applied is a core function of leadership. If there is a disconnect between the application or whether the rule is true to stated values, leaders also need to speak truth to power and push for change.

Engage Constructively

A critical part of being a positive leader involves supporting colleagues and seeking out solutions. Breweries are complex workspaces, comprising a blend of mechanical equipment, biochemical processes, supply chain management, and personalities. Equipment breaks, schedules change at the last minute, and mistakes happen.

When problems crop up, it is easy to view them purely through a negative lens: nothing ever works around here, they never listen, we're going to be left holding the bag, etc. All of that may be true, but none of it will address the underlying situation. Effective leaders focus on what can be done to resolve the issue instead of fixating on the problem or who is

LEADERSHIP: DELIVERING CONSISTENT MESSAGING

- Walk the walk: your actions and behavior are more impactful than any speech.
- Acknowledge your mistakes publicly: being open about the error, the impact, and the resolution are signs of respect, not weakness.
- Admit when you don't know something.
- Seek out and listen to feedback: what you said can be different than what people heard.
- Take notes and share them with other stakeholders: successful operations depend on a common pool of knowledge.
- Decisions need to stand on their own merits: even the appearance of favoritism is corrosive, so the decision-making process needs to be clearly defined and data driven.

to blame for a situation. Note that this doesn't mean pretending that all is well: problems aren't resolved by ignoring them, especially when they involve interpersonal issues.

By engaging with their teams and seeking resolutions, effective leaders help give their colleagues agency. Instead of feeling like bystanders, team members should have a way to actively work out the problem, which is beneficial both operationally and from the perspective of morale. No one enjoys feeling like a cog in an unfeeling machine. Leadership helps address that by creating a space for active participation.

Mentoring and Coaching Colleagues

Active participation isn't limited to handling conflicts or emergencies. Supporting peers by helping them develop professionally is a central role for positive leadership. Every employee has their own professional journey, regardless of whether they're actively involved in a formal development process.

How your core values get translated into action is where establishing a set of priorities becomes crucial. Simply being told that something is important

LEADERSHIP: ENGAGING WITH YOUR TEAMS

- Control your emotions: complaining about a situation isn't the same as advocating for change; venting is an entirely normal response, but there is a time and place.
- Focus on solutions: negativity is contagious and doesn't solve anything. Look for what can be done, not what can't.
- Put in the work to prepare and plan: saying that an idea "should" work is a dodge. Explain what you expect to happen and how you'll adapt if things don't go according to plan.
- Listen to your team: address their concerns and explain your own thought process.

isn't the same as knowing how to put those ideas into practice. When this is left undefined, people will supply their own definitions, drawing from previous experience and what they see around them. Having leaders demonstrate core values on a consistent basis is important for any employee, doubly so for new staff. Clear examples like this set the standard for how your employees interact with the workspace, their tasks, and most importantly, their colleagues.

The challenge for leaders is that modeling behaviors, on its own, is a passive approach: it depends on people picking up on those cues and adopting the desired behaviors on their own. Mentoring and coaching are active approaches to reinforcing values and expectations.

No matter how thorough the training cycle, you can't cover everything in a 60- or 90-day period. The daily implementation of knowledge over time is what cements that material into memory and lived practice. Through mentorship and coaching, leaders work as extensions of the training process. In either role, the goal of an effective leader doesn't change: invest time and energy in people to help them live up to their potential.

Mentorship can be thought of as being an active guide on how to operate successfully within the brewery by helping employees better understand their duties and preparing them for future opportunities. Mentors serve as resources for their peers, whether they're new to the brewery or experienced team members transitioning into new roles and responsibilities. This may take the form of being a sounding board for questions, regularly checking in on colleagues, or demonstrating best practices. This needs to be an active process. Don't assume that people will always bring their questions to you—leaders have a responsibility to reach out. Fundamentally, mentoring employees is an exercise in developing the next generation of talent within the organization by serving as a support system for them.

Coaching has a different role, which is to be a proactive teacher to employees, bringing a specific focus on a skill or topic. This role can involve teaching new skills or it can be a way to ensure employees remain strong in the fundamentals.

A coach might work to prepare an employee for a new role or challenge by providing opportunities to introduce and teach new skills. In this context, coaching is literally the act of putting professional development into practice for an employee and helping carve out resources like time and attention for them. Alternatively, coaching can help with friction points that are affecting job performance by identifying and addressing the root causes. In most cases, people don't come to work thinking, "I want to cause problems or make mistakes." Some form of disconnect is involved. The role of the coach here is work with the employee to identify the disconnect, getting back to fundamentals and clarifying issues, whether that involves a technical process or illustrating how values and behaviors affect team dynamics.

These aspects of leadership will come up again later in the book, but the takeaway here is that an employee's learning on the job is an ongoing, active process. The emphasis has to start during the orientation and training phases, but it does not and cannot stop there. Leaders have to play an active role here. Talking about the importance of safety in a slide presentation isn't as powerful as bringing it up consistently throughout the training process and reinforcing it through demonstrating this behavior to the rest of the team.

LEADERSHIP: MENTORING AND COACHING

- It's not about you: start with the assumption that people are operating in good faith and adjust your approach to help them understand what is being asked of them.
- Be available to your team: if they don't feel comfortable approaching you, they won't.
- Connect the dots: breweries are complex spaces, so take the time to consistently point out the *why* behind tasks and how the team fits into the overall operation.
- Break down tasks into small steps and focus on how to do them successfully. Emphasizing two or three key habits will be more successful than walking an employee through what not to do.
- Don't be a helicopter parent: people need space to work through complications on their own.

MANAGEMENT ROLES AND FUNCTIONS

Where leadership is about inspiration, management is about accountability—is the organization and its staff walking the walk? As stated at the beginning of this chapter, leadership and management can go hand in hand, but they are separate tracks.

Management is a very specific but frequently misunderstood skill set. To understand it better, let's start with what it isn't: management isn't the reduction of the brewery into equations and spreadsheets or punishments and promotions. Effective teams will certainly look closely at metrics, but these are indicators, not the underlying reality. Metrics and patterns offer a glimpse into operations but the core of every brewery is still its people who perform their tasks each and every day.

The role of the manager is to foster effective teams through accountability. This has several components at the individual, team, and organizational levels, but there are common features throughout: set expectations, manage to those expectations, and reduce friction to support your people.

Any expectation in the brewery needs to be grounded in a tangible factor that genuinely matters to the overall health of the organization. These may be performance-related, such as maximizing the amount of quality beer produced, but successful organizations also need to pay attention to behavioral factors. No matter how talented an employee may be at their listed job duties, problematic behavior has costs that shouldn't be ignored. A pattern of not supporting the overall team drains morale and energy from the whole. Left unchecked, even the best recipe development or record sales placements won't outweigh an employee's problem behavior driving their peers out of the brewery (and potentially the entire industry).

Set Individual Goals and Manage Performance

Just as successful safety and quality programs start at the individual level, so does management. There are two essential criteria for individual expectations: job performance and employment expectations. At the most basic level, expectations should be recognizable in the job description for the position. This is the document that laid out what you were hiring for and what they signed on for, so if expectations aren't clear from the start, you're starting on the back foot.

WORKPLACE EXPECTATIONS AND INTERACTIONS

Workplace expectations differ from job performance expectations in that they involve how individuals interact with their colleagues. Employee handbooks often try to categorize and define these interactions but struggle with the sheer variety. Anyone who has been in a management role for long will have experienced situations that cause you to think to yourself, "I never thought I would have to explain that to an adult. What were they thinking?!" At their most basic level these expectations center around respect. How teammates interact with each other can make or break a team. Holding people to account for their actions is essential.

Orientation and training are the next steps once a new employee is hired. These phases should be designed to provide a deep dive into job performance expectations and place these in the context of brewery operations as a whole. Once you declare that an employee has completed their training pipeline, you're signifying that they understand the tasks and responsibilities of their position. From there, the challenge is maintaining that edge. Familiarity can lead to complacency if you're not careful.

Set Team Goals and Manage Performance

Everyone will end up having the occasional bad day, but having a robust team around them will help soften the effects and protect the overall objectives for the day. This requires management to step back from individual tasks and look at the big picture. What are the goals, what are the priorities, and how do you keep everything on track?

There are several ways to accomplish this, and most of them revolve around creating structures. These help to provide consistency over time and allow for accurate comparisons. Management by anecdote is vulnerable to the whims and assumptions of your staff: stable growth demands a more stable foundation.

One approach is to develop and monitor key performance indicators (KPIs). These metrics help steer performance assessments toward fact-based measurements that can be compared over time. KPIs are designed to be objective: the numbers are what they are. The challenge is going through the results, identifying causes, and making adjustments. To perform this investigative work consistently and fairly, you need to have good numbers. Once KPIs are set, they need to be introduced to the team. If the team does not understand the KPIs they are being measured on, they will not understand feedback about them.

Managing schedules is another core management function that benefits from structure. The obvious part is developing and assigning shifts and start times to employees, but the deeper function is matching people to tasks. What experience and skill sets need to be available? How many people will be required to provide enough coverage to complete the task and still allow for breaks, meals, or unscheduled absences?

EXAMPLES OF KEY PERFORMANCE INDICATORS

Safety
- Incident rates—type per period metric
  - Types
    - Recordable injuries
    - Near misses
  - Metric
    - Per quarter
    - Per operational area (e.g., beer production, beer packaging, tap room/hospitality)
    - Per labor hours worked
    - Per barrel produced

Quality
- Quality holds per quarter
  - Missed specifications, microbiological holds, DO measurements, seam checks, etc.
  - Priority given to holds that delay releasing beer to market

Efficiency
- Brewhouse efficiency
- Packaging efficiency
  - Beer volume
  - Packaging material loss
- Maintenance work orders
  - Issued versus cleared
  - Maintenance-related schedule changes
- Labor hours per barrel (packaged volume)

Schedules benefit from a clear sense of what tasks are involved. Having a checklist for opening and closing duties for each shift provides a useful guiderail that addresses what needs to be done and whether the assigned staff has the requisite skills or authorities. A brewer can help set up a taproom prior to opening, but they probably haven't been trained on setting up the cash drawer or running the point-of-sale system; likewise, a bartender can lend a hand in the brewery but generally isn't trained on harvesting and pitching yeast.

RECOGNIZING WHERE THE PAIN IS COMING FROM

Industry veteran Jim Helmke used to tell a story about distinguishing between situations that capture the headlines versus those that are actually causing damage. In this case, a high-speed rotary filler malfunctioned and halted a packaging line for several hours. After getting the equipment back up and running, his packaging manager and maintenance manager had a long and contentious meeting about the cause and accompanying responsibility.

Rather than assigning blame, Helmke assigned another employee to monitor the filler and log every incident of the filler stopping during a run for more than a few minutes. After a month of monitoring, they tallied the results and found that these short-duration stoppages added up to far more lost time than the incident that drew so much attention and drama.

The point of the story was to highlight that focusing on high-profile incidents tends to draw attention away from situations that are less obvious but more damaging. Major equipment malfunctions commanded an enormous amount of attention and resources but were relatively rare. The short stoppages, on the other hand, were barely noticed but it turned out they caused more lost time and quality variability. And this pattern of short duration stoppages was happening month after month with zero fanfare.

Now compare that to interpersonal conflicts. Fistfights and assaults are rare, but casual disrespect and microaggressions do happen every day. Leaders and managers need to recognize problems early and engage with them where they occur. Waiting until a problem flares up is too late.

Looking at the demands of the production schedule or taproom calendar over a multiweek time horizon is essential when balancing time off requests. It also enables you to know where there is flexibility for important events such as training opportunities and maintenance work.

DEVELOPING LEADERS AND MANAGERS

The most important idea behind creating a leadership and management team is to recognize that you always want to be training your successors. Having a deep bench is critical for being successful in the long term. Managers who withhold knowledge or opportunities in an effort to be indispensable or irreplaceable, even if unconsciously, are impeding growth and leaving the brewery vulnerable to disruptions. Even at the personal level, being able to go on vacation or take sick time without work interruptions should be seen as a net positive.

Leadership as a Learned Skill

Leadership is a learned skill and is something you can nurture in your brewery. This starts by actively identifying the people viewed as leaders within the organization. These people include both the formal and informal leaders: if their peers see them as role models, they're leaders. The first step in the process of reinforcing positive leadership is making those you have identified aware of their impact within the brewery—they may not recognize how they are viewed. You also need to address negative behavior. Leaders don't always have a positive impact, and that needs to be nipped in the bud. Experienced team members can be incredibly valuable mentors and repositories of knowledge, but they can also undermine even the best SOPs and training cycles with the phrase "but this is how we do things." Charisma also plays a significant role. Regardless of how long someone has worked at the brewery, force of personality can exert an influence on how others behave, for better or worse.

Once you've identified leaders, you have a responsibility to support them. The easiest form of this is to check in regularly with them. Leadership carries an emotional weight that people aren't necessarily prepared for: becoming aware that colleagues are looking to your example is a genuine burden. Providing peer support is important. Trading best practices and being sounding

NAVIGATING DIFFICULT CONVERSATIONS

Addressing performance errors or behavioral issues with colleagues is rarely easy, but these conversations need to be productive. How you go about them matters. Note that these points apply to everyone in a conversation, including managers: don't carry your own baggage into an unrelated situation.

- The world is bigger than just the brewery: recognize that these conversations can feel more high stakes than you intend.
  - Don't sandbag people: pick a time and place that will be conducive to an actual conversation.
  - Stressors exist inside and outside of the brewery, and they affect how messages are heard.
  - Disagreements can feel threatening: be prepared to deescalate the situation. This may involve taking a break to reduce the tension but start by reinforcing the actual stakes and goals of the conversation.
- Explanations and descriptions should be fact-based.
  - Implying intentions can trigger defensiveness, so focus on facts as they are.
  - Put time into finding out as much as you can about the situation before starting the conversation. Incorrect assumptions only make a difficult conversation worse.
  - Actively listen to what is being said and consider the implications: employees may have legitimate reasons for their actions.
- A useful set of questions to consider during a conversation are:
  - *What do I not know about the situation?* —Give people an opportunity to explain where they are coming from.
  - *What else may be true?* —It's easy to make assumptions; be open to being wrong about them.
- End with clarity
  - Recap the facts that were discussed.
  - Give them a chance to ask questions.
  - Define the expectations, next steps, and any timelines.

boards for each other helps the transition; and creating a safe space for leaders to talk about the experience is useful no matter how long they've been in the role.

Investing in training leaders on how to effectively mentor and coach other employees pays significant dividends. Breweries can seek out formal development courses and opportunities, both within the brewing community and from other sectors, but home-grown programs can be a strong return on investment if you put some thought into them. Existing leaders need to make time to mentor the next generation.

The simple act of previewing policy or process changes with leaders before rolling them out to the wider team has advantages. It's not that leaders are more important than others, but they are going to be the ones that people go to for answers to questions. Change can be hard, so providing them with information on what is happening and why it matters goes a long way toward understanding and acceptance.

Another critical skill is spending time practicing difficult conversations with other leaders. Even for people who are naturally gifted at this, it is a skill that benefits from practice. It can feel artificial to roleplay these scenarios, but the act of doing it reveals where you are most uncomfortable and need to devote time and practice.

Management Training

Leaders play a huge part in establishing team dynamics through their work ethic and mentorship. Unfortunately, there are limits to just demonstrating job performance. Peer pressure can provide a nudge, but if employees aren't picking up what their teammates are laying down then an intervention needs to occur. This is the role of the manager.

In many organizations, becoming a manager is seen as the natural next step for someone particularly gifted in their role or who has been with the company for several years. The problem with this approach is that managing people and budgets is not the same as coordinating yeast management in the cellar or smoothly navigating a busy night behind the tap-room bar. Promoting staff from their strengths and comfort zones into a management position without adequately preparing them does a disservice to the entire team. Building an employee's managerial skill set is essential if they are to be an effective manager. A necessary component for gaining these skills involves organic development: senior leadership needs to provide mentorship and coaching to these new managers.

Coaching opportunities include tasking prospective managers with leading pre-shift huddles and organizing small projects, such as conducting month-end inventories and comparing the results against production logs or setting up training for a new beer release with serving staff. Whatever the project, the goals here are to introduce new and prospective managers to the role of coordinating groups of people around a specific goal and having a clear sense of accountability.

The mentorship portion is immensely valuable. Management has a significant learning curve, so sharing knowledge and experience with newly minted managers helps to smooth the learning curve. Mentors also serve to reinforce core values by providing a sense of institutional knowledge and memory to newer peers. Being able to learn from previous situations and challenges helps new managers apply core values across a variety of scenarios that they haven't personally experienced and still be consistent with previous practice.

A word of caution does need to be mentioned here, however: managers live within a workplace culture, not outside of it. Their behaviors can live up to stated core values or be contrary to them. Mentorship from managers who overlook problems within the brewery will perpetuate negative behaviors into the next generation.

More formal education and training can come from outside the brewery through management-focused seminars at industry and non-industry conferences. However management skills are learned, it is important to connect those to the brewery environment. Placing knowledge into context is essential to successful adoption.

Key Skills for Managers

The role of manager involves a blend of high-level understanding of business operations with day-to-day running of the floor. Managers are expected to know what is good for the brewery financially and be able to report trends to leadership, while also coordinating teams in a way that keeps the brewery running smoothly and promotes employee work-life balance. This requires a wide range of skills that, at times, may seem impossible to summarize. We'll look at the following key skills that are an essential part of a manager's role:

- Understanding the business as a whole
  - Financial literacy: understanding COGS and other factors
  - How does the brewery make money?
  - What do customers expect from the brewery?
- Writing schedules
- Performance and conflict management
- Running meetings – This forms a key part of employee engagement, so we take a look at this topic in chapter 6 (p. 90).

Understanding the Business and Financial Literacy

Managers have greater access and exposure to the financial side of the brewery by virtue of their position. Understanding how the brewery makes money is an important part of being able to manage processes and people. Not every activity generates the same amount of revenue, and revenue isn't the same as profitability. If managers are expected to prevent loss and help the brewery make money, financial literacy is needed.

Balancing financial opportunities and pressures is central to the role of manager. Owners and senior managers need to spend time familiarizing new and junior managers with the basic financials of the brewery so that the latter can make informed decisions about what to prioritize on a daily or weekly basis. Three simple but significant metrics include:

- Cost of goods sold (COGS)—control costs and recognize sources of loss.
- Labor costs per barrel sold (production) or daily sales (hospitality)—make the best use of your staff's time.
- Product mixes (sales by brand by SKU/serving size)—understand which beers are actually paying the bills so that you can control where you focus your efforts.

Learning about financial factors starts the process, but the larger return on investment comes from periodic reviews of these metrics between managers and senior leadership. These reviews can vary from weekly to annual sessions. Regardless of the frequency, the core purpose is to identify and address financial factors, just as you would with safety or quality issues with your beers. Managers may need to address excess material waste or pay more attention to how they schedule staff.

Writing Schedules

Writing schedules is a core management function. Schedules can be tricky, particularly in hospitality environments like taprooms, kitchens, or events. As the manager responsible, you need the right number of people working at the right time with the right skills to complete the necessary tasks. Managers need to understand several factors in order to be effective:

- Tasks and realistic expectations—what needs to be accomplished and what does the timeframe look like?
- Skill sets required for a shift or project—who will be needed?
- Time requirements for that expertise—when and how long do you need those people?
- Flexibility and realistic workflows, e.g., scheduling breaks and other rotations
- Managing costs and work-life balance. Being overstaffed will reduce wages for taproom employees and increase costs in production, while being understaffed too often will lead to burnout.

Labor costs compared against monthly production or sales provides an overview of how efficient you are with scheduling staff and coordinating workflows. These trends can be analyzed (or not), but the main role of managers is to utilize labor effectively in real time. Reports will tell you what happened but being effective happens in the moment. Factors to consider include:

- Coordinating staff rotations
  - Schedule breaks and lunches whenever possible, but the key is to communicate with employees to make sure they have the opportunity to take them.
  - For tasks that involve significant repetitive motion, rotating people through workstations will reduce the potential for injury.

- Communicating tasks
  - Pre-shift meetings are ideal for laying out the workflow for the day.
  - Checklists are effective for keeping track of routine tasks.
  - Dry-erase boards are excellent at facilitating communication about the status of daily or weekly project lists between staff.
  - Managers can review these task lists and re-prioritize them as needed.
- Assigning tasks and setting expectations
  - A simple example is assigning a team member to a specific task (e.g., using a deck brush to clean an area or having a set of jockey boxes cleaned) or coordinating a larger group effort such as reorganizing a storage area.
  - Occasionally, people will need some direction on what tasks to perform next; ideally, this is a subtle nudge to check the task board. Other circumstances will call for a more direct reminder that there are still open tasks that need to be completed. Having the messaging being about the effect on the team is generally the most effective, but if a habit is developing, addressing it as a performance issue early is better than letting it continue.

Performance and Conflict Management

Managing performance is a key component of the manager's role. Leaders are called upon to inspire, but when core values are being violated, managers need to step in. Enforcing brewery values, standards, and policies is fundamental to a healthy, functioning workplace culture. This starts with setting an example with your own behavior, but managers must also review process logs, observe interpersonal interactions, and monitor workplace behavior. When employee actions don't live up to the expectations that have been set, these issues need to be addressed. Chapter 4 covers performance assessment broadly, but managers need to be trained and prepared for professional conflicts.

Handling conflicts can be adversarial, but they don't need to be. Earlier in the chapter we laid out a set of guidelines for navigating difficult conversations (p. 79). These practices don't eliminate tensions, but they do help guide the conversation to a more effective outcome. Avoiding conflict or a difficult discussion because it is uncomfortable will only exacerbate problems.

A best practice for these situations is to conduct them with another manager or leader present. The purpose of a second manager isn't to gang up on an employee. Rather, their role is to help keep the discussion productive and act as a circuit breaker in the event of tensions rising. This is a major reason why we have emphasized the importance of building trust: if staff don't feel that they'll be heard and respected, employees are unlikely to participate fully and assume the worst.

Preparing managers for this function can be difficult. This is another reason for having an additional manager present in conflicts: this is a prime opportunity for coaching and mentorship. Experienced managers need to support their junior peers, discussing both the approach in advance and reviewing the outcome afterward. In addition, the second manager can serve as the point of contact for following up with the employee and offer mentorship to them as well. Effective cultures are dependent on their teams, so approaching behavior in a collective manner is superior to individual interactions.

CULTURE AS AN ORGANIZATIONAL EFFORT

So far, we have been talking about organizational culture in the abstract, looking at the various components necessary for a healthy and resilient workspace, from hiring and training new employees to professional development and leadership and managerial skills. At some point, however, the rubber has to hit the road: the organizational culture within your brewery needs to be a lived experience. And have no doubt, your brewery has an active culture within the staff, potentially more than one depending on the number of discrete teams in the organization. The question is whether that is the culture you intended to promote.

Developing and fostering a viable organizational culture needs to be a series of intentional acts. Some acts will be large, others small, but these efforts have to be made every day. Culture is not a spectator sport. Like safety and quality, culture is defined by *what you do*. Your actions, your decisions, these are the organizing principles of workplace culture. As the author Adam Fridman describes it, "Purpose is about why we do what we do, values are how we achieve purpose. Habits are what we do every day that reflects our

purpose and values. Habits are purpose and values made visible."[1] The challenge for every brewery is breathing life into the fundamentals we covered in the first five chapters. As always, it helps to apply some structure and develop a plan.

MODELING ENGAGEMENT

Ultimately, breweries have two identities. The first identity comes from the entrepreneurial vision of the founders. The second identity is best described as what consumers think of when they think of the brand. Ideally, those descriptions should mesh, but accomplishing that comes down to execution. Performing tasks correctly is what leads to high-quality beer, positive consumer experiences, and financial stability.

Gorgeous aesthetics and top-notch equipment will attract attention, but repeat business and recommendations are driven by positive interactions, whether those are with taproom staff or the sensory experience from the beers themselves. This is the realm of organizational culture—when workplaces are stressed, under-resourced, or unprepared, those experiences will suffer.

[1] Adam Fridman, "Four Essential Habits to Align Purpose and Values With Actions: Purpose Inspires. Values Guide. Habits Define," *Inc.*, June 15, 2017, https://www.inc.com/adam-fridman/four-essential-habits-to-align-purpose-and-values-with-actions.html.

Planning for Growth: Proactively Mapping Out Requirement and Objectives

Business planning factors

Barrelage targets: Years 1, 3, 5
- Year 1: 600 bbl.
- Year 3: 1,500 bbl.
- Year 5: 4,600 bbl.

Production CAPEX: Budgets and equipment
- When do critical investments get made to reach those targets?
- Increased volume: additional FV/BBT, packaging upgrades
- Minimizing waste: QA/QC investments, centrifuges

Costing projections
- Managing COGS and labor costs/barrel

VS

Cultural planning factors

Staffing: Priorities and contingency planning
- Hiring
  - What skills do we need?
  - Where should we be recruiting?
  - When do we make key hires? (e.g., a dedicated maintenance technician or events coordinator)
- Shifts and flexibility
  - Setting reasonable expectations
- Turnover versus retention
  - Being prepared for turnover
  - Making sure that we retain critical personnel

Resources and benefits
- What changes can we accomplish as resources become available?
- What do teams need to be supported?
  - Spare parts, tools, consistent management and communication, etc.
- What do individuals need for support?
  - PTO, flexibility, constructive feedback, etc.
- Are these accessible and sustainable?
  - Never be in a position that a benefit has to be withdrawn because headcount growth has made it "too expensive."

Training and development programs
- Year 1—Establish SOPs
  - Emphasize sensory and quality assurance checks
- Year 3—Develop redundant skill sets across the team
  - Schedule cross-training and opportunities for staff to spend a shift with colleagues from other teams to better understand they challenges they face.
  - Set aside funds for conferences, defraying membership costs to professional industry organizations, etc.
- Year 5—Connect with legacy
  - Encourage cross-departmental engagement

Figure 6.1. Business plans typically focus on financial metrics around production and sales. Managing that growth smoothly requires investing time in thinking through personnel and cultural components.

Laying out a plan for cultural development is a powerful complement to the traditional business plan. Concrete metrics for the financial health and viability of the organization are undeniably necessary, but the subtleties arise when you ask how well will the business plan translate into customer experience. Rather than looking at financial metrics and objectives, a culture plan will aim to describe the conditions necessary for building effective teams and empowering employees to do their best work. Wherever there is a revenue- or volume-based objective that triggers a new round of growth or investment, there needs to be a corresponding plan that lays out how that growth will be supported and sustained in the workspace (fig. 6.1).

In chapter 5, we looked at how leadership and management intersect within the brewery. Leadership and management are responsible for setting the conditions that give rise to the desired cultural attributes. Leadership offers up both a vision and a consistent, active example of what the organization strives for and rewards. Management focuses on providing employees with the necessary resources and tools to accomplish those aims.

We discussed a brewery's core resources in the introduction: time, money, and attention. A significant aspect of building a successful culture involves providing enough of each. Money is a function of budgeting for the necessary cashflow at the right time. Time is frequently defined as money, but there are additional dimensions. Many worthy initiatives falter when there isn't sufficient time allocated to doing the project without impeding operations or burning out staff. Attention is more subtle. When tasks start to feel like busywork, it can be difficult to muster up the motivation to perform the work on a regular basis. No matter how important the task or the amount of time and money assigned to it, if leaders don't engage and follow up on the results, that lack of attention starts to signal that it's busywork and progress will stumble.

Reinforcing this sense of attention is where a cultural framework comes into play. By creating opportunities for engagement, you demonstrate to employees how projects and tasks are valued across the brewery. The options for how to do this vary as widely as do the needs of individual breweries, but there are common factors that we will discuss here.

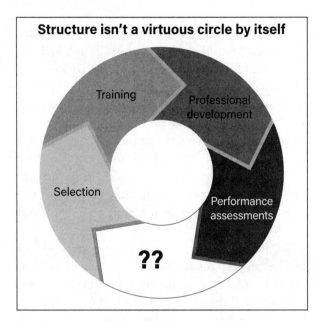

Figure 6.2. The components of building workplace cultures aren't simply a series of boxes to be checked off. In order to be effective, they have to serve a broader set of goals.

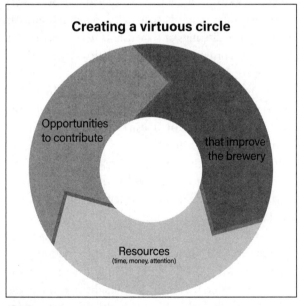

Figure 6.3. Effective cultures develop feedback loops with objectives that create the conditions for continued growth. Each component prepares the building blocks for iterative steps toward successful outcomes.

ANATOMY OF ENGAGEMENT

To be successful, the components of your cultural framework need to satisfy three basic conditions: balance, connection, and follow-through. Each of these conditions play a role in reinforcing values and strengthening the organization.

Providing Balance

Brewery work is an exercise in multitasking and managing priorities. A small brewery will have a correspondingly small staff where everyone must wear multiple hats throughout the workweek. Introducing new projects or programs tends to carry a risk of adding burdens to an already busy team. There is often an unspoken minimum for the number of expected hours spent in the brewery or working on brewery tasks, and that minimum often comes without a corresponding maximum. If work-life balance is expected to mean something, there needs to be boundaries. Pay structures that imply 40-hour weeks aren't consistent with workflows that regularly lead to 60-hour weeks.

Designing workflows that avoid burnout is essential to a successful launch and sustained engagement. There are several strategies for accomplishing this. First and foremost, be realistic about how long planning and implementation will take and match that up against your existing work schedules. Never underestimate the planning stage: working and thinking through requirements will help to reduce scheduling conflicts and identify the personnel and skill sets needed in advance.

Managers need to carve out dedicated times to actively work on new projects. Tasks that simply get piled onto existing workloads tend to get bumped in favor of daily production needs. Even when such tasks are successfully added to the workflow, there is a labor cost associated with the additional hours and a social cost affixed to the additional demand on the employees' schedules. This latter point is particularly true for salaried staff, but it applies to everyone in the brewery.

Building in dedicated time may extend the implementation of a project, but the work produced will generally be superior. Avoiding burnout also helps to avoid operators coming to resent a project or initiative. Having an implementation phase that feels starved of resources only increases the existing challenge, even when the actual eventual outcome would be a benefit to employees and make their work lives better.

Creating Connections

A healthy organizational culture develops a strong network of relationships to help reinforce shared values. When employees feel disconnected from their peers or the overall direction of the brewery, it becomes difficult to stay motivated and engaged. Developing a common sense of purpose is critical to long-term success and creating an equitable working environment; active leadership and management are essential to this process (see p. 73).

To foster a sense of connection, employees need to feel that they are genuinely part of the brewery. Coming in and punching a timecard isn't the same thing as participating. This doesn't mean that decisions are decided through an open free-for-all discussion or company-wide consensus. Rather, the goal is to allow employees the license to express themselves and contribute ideas. Having ideas bubble up from the people closest to daily operations can lead to improvements in safety, quality, and efficiency, all of which contribute directly to a better bottom line financially. A top-down structure can cut itself off from these opportunities if the culture signals to employees that they should keep their heads down and do what they're told.

Creating a culture of feedback can happen through a variety of means. Regularly checking in with employees offers a quick way to invite suggestions, while pre-shift huddles and other team meetings should always feature an opportunity for employees to offer up ideas (pp. 58–60). Better yet, leaders should actively solicit feedback from their colleagues—encouraging input is hugely important and more effective than passively waiting for ideas.

This communication can happen face-to-face or through written means. For example, a common feature among breweries that use collaborative messaging software systems like Slack is having chat rooms dedicated to pitching ideas for new beers, brand names, operational suggestions, and other issues facing the brewery. Even the classic suggestion box provides a format for staff to drop a note and communicate their ideas.

The corollary to encouraging feedback is devoting time to reviewing and acknowledging the material. Effective communication is predicated on trust, and when employees feel that no one is listening, they'll stop talking.

Recognizing good ideas is also part of fostering a sense of connection. Employees who feel that they are part of the success of the brewery is an important part of making strong team bonds. This takes several forms. First, being publicly recognized and appreciated for contributions in front of peers directly helps

morale, both for the individual and the wider team. The second form is knowing about events and successes that involve the brewery in the wider world. There is a sense of pride that comes with recognition from others. Success may be winning awards, positive news stories about a brewery initiative, or learning that the brewery just picked up several new accounts. This is doubly true for remote workers: employees finding out from social media that the brewery won an award or just tapped a brand-new beer rather than hearing the news from their own employer is a recipe for disconnection.

Techniques for establishing these connections all revolve around communication. Making a point to mention brewery wins during team meetings is one avenue. Another is to use the messaging functionality built into various productivity software platforms to broadcast news in near-real time.[2] Publishing an internal newsletter is more old-school but has a lot of upsides. Even if newsletters are relatively curated lists of brewery news, they offer more space to talk about events and can include press clippings or screenshots from other media.

Regular communication also helps to avoid the creation of information silos. These tend to develop within teams or departments and inhibit the spread of information. This can have several consequences. First, useful information doesn't make it into the hands of others who will be affected by it. Diagnosing (or better yet, preventing) problems is made more difficult when information is kept from other stakeholders. This can happen deliberately when people function as gatekeepers, but more commonly it happens because it doesn't occur to people that someone else may need to know about a particular piece of information.

Another form of siloing is lack of awareness about how teams operate. From the outside, working a bar shift doesn't look that hard. On the sales side, many assume that brewery representatives basically just visit bars and drink beer for a living. Those misconceptions would fall apart the moment people spent a day working alongside them. Proximity is common in small and newly opened breweries, but disconnect starts to creep in as organizations grow and mature. Periodically bringing groups together into cross-departmental teams, even if it is just to talk about their work over beers periodically, helps to prevent silos

---

2   Productivity platforms such as Slack or Microsoft Teams allow for threads, while scheduling software like Restaurant365 allow for frequent, easy (but one-way) communication to share news across entire teams.

from forming. These cross-departmental conversations are relatively common among managers because coordination across teams is part of their job, but this doesn't necessarily filter down to line staff. Fostering such opportunities makes a significant difference by creating a sense of teamwork across departments.

WORDS OF WISDOM

I spoke to Laura Mullen, Vice President of Outreach and Events at Bent Paddle Brewery, about the brewery's approach to teambuilding through good staff communications.

Teambuilding

Bent Paddle Brewery holds quarterly staff meetings. Some start with a business-focused meeting and then shift to just allowing staff to interact outside of the brewery; others skip the business portion entirely and just focus on employees relaxing. Bent Paddle has brewery, warehouse, and taproom staff spread across three different buildings, plus remote sales representatives, so many employees don't work closely together on a daily or even weekly basis. Creating a space for employees to come together is an important part of maintaining a common bond.

Prior to COVID-19, these quarterly meetings were retreats or field trips, frequently overnight or weekend trips. The brewery has kept trips closer to home lately, but regardless of the location or format, all of these meetings start the same way: having each employee state their best personal and professional experiences since the last gathering. Sharing accomplishments is an important part of building camaraderie and connections. While Bent Paddle does pay attention to the cost of teambuilding exercises, it measures the return on investment through how engaged the employees are with the activities. Getting people outside and spending time with one another is the core focus, one in keeping with the brewery's identity and mission.

These meetings are also about transparency and putting a human face on the brewery. During the January all-staff meeting, employees offer up their personal and professional bests from the previous year, while ownership shares a performance dashboard with the entire company. This dashboard includes information on a broad range of topics. Some of these are confidential, but the brewery's leadership trusts its team. Other items are informational and give a sense of scale and the big picture, while others are just goofy and fun.

Dashboard Material

(Kindly provided by L. Mullen, Bent Paddle Brewery.)

Personnel
- Number of employees
- Diversity metrics

Volume
- Barrels sold
- Pounds of malt and hops used
- Number of cans packed and sold

Financials
- A basic profit and loss statement: total revenue minus COGS and operating costs

Sales
- Total number of sales accounts with a distribution territory map
- Breakdown of sales by brand

Taproom
- Pints poured
- Number of flights poured
- Number of tours
- Number of live bands and events
- Social media impressions

Impact of Paddle It Forward (Bent Paddle's charitable arm)
- Charitable donations
- Number of events

Snapshot of Goals for Next Year
- Core initiatives and targets
- Key investments
- New product launches

RUNNING A SUCCESSFUL MEETING

One of the more reliable truisms in the business world is that meetings generally suck. They take us away from our actual work, frequently don't have any clear purpose, and nothing useful comes out of them. Thinking about meetings through the lens of engagement can help address these issues.

Balance

- **Respect people's time:** start meetings on time and end them on time.
  - A meeting's duration should reflect its agenda.
  - Tangents are a time suck: call these out in real time and stick to the plan. It's not about being the fun police, it's about staying on track.
- **People are policy:** having the right mix of attendees is a key factor for success.
  - Without the appropriate decision-makers in the room, progress can stall.
  - Bringing anyone and everyone into a meeting is a waste of time for people who aren't involved in the discussion.

Connection

- **Focus on business priorities.**
  - Meetings should be targeted at issues that are affecting the business.
  - Work on the issues that are causing problems, not pet peeves.
- **The purpose of each meeting should be clear.**
  - Know the objective: What needs to be decided or shared?
  - Define the next steps: What outcomes are required?
  - It is helpful to apply the SMART mnemonic: Specific, Measurable, Attainable, Relevant, Timely
- **Form follows function:** tailor the meeting format to the objective.
  - Brainstorming benefits from a freewheeling format, whereas process planning demands more structure. Prepare your agenda and expectations accordingly—trying to impose a single meeting style onto every situation can lead to frustration.

- **Expect people to arrive prepared.**
  - Meetings are expected to have a purpose, and attendees need to be ready to participate.
  - Preparation does take time, so allow personnel sufficient time to be ready.
    - Create task- or topic-specific working groups to develop information and options in advance.

Follow-Through

- **Meetings should have clear outcomes:** define the tasks needed for the next steps.
  - Identify specific action items.
  - Determine who is performing those action items.
  - Establish deadlines for action items but be realistic about timelines and existing workloads.
- **Create common knowledge:** meeting notes are a mechanism for accountability.
  - Information needs to be documented and shared across the team.
  - Accuracy matters, so provide a review period and distribute any corrections or additions.
- **Make use of working groups to continue acting on meeting results.**
  - Not everything has to happen during a single meeting—make good use of the subject matter experts within your teams.
- **Meeting overruns:** if the working agenda can't be completed during the allotted timeframe, settle on a plan appropriate to whatever outcomes are required.
  - Extend the meeting
  - Table discussion until a future meeting
  - Delegate to a working group and update the larger team when ready

Follow-Through

Even the best-intentioned programs will suffer if they don't produce results. Management has to deliver on promises made in order to be seen as acting in good faith. What is said isn't nearly as important as what eventually happens. This is a two-way street between leadership and employees at large: in order for accountability to be effective, everyone has to play their part. However, when individuals or specific teams fall short on an initiative, the first review should focus on whether they were provided with sufficient resources by the leadership or management.

Establishing action items helps to set the conditions for effective follow-through. Action items may come out of team meetings or informal conversations, but the idea is the same: What needs to happen, who is going to perform the work, and when does it need to be completed? In practice, organizations tend to be fairly good at the first point, touch on the second, and overlook the deadline portion. Getting all three of these components right makes a huge difference, however.

Future discussions or meetings benefit from looking back at open action items. The result may be to quickly mark them off as "completed"

SNATCHING DEFEAT FROM THE JAWS OF VICTORY

Change can be difficult to embrace, even in the good times. Any small change from the status quo can feel disruptive, particularly when staff feel that something has been taken from them. Changes to benefits such as paid time off or health insurance policies have effects that extend well beyond the brewery and are intensely personal. Paying attention to how programs are rolled out makes a huge difference between teams recognizing the benefits of an update versus fixating on the change itself.

Prepare the field

Take the time to explain upcoming policy changes to the staff: what is changing, how does it affect/benefit employees, and why you are making this change. With revisions to areas such as health coverage, think about the full range of stakeholders. Spouses or partners may have specific questions, so holding informational sessions outside of traditional work hours opens up the process to them. Bringing stakeholders into the fold from the beginning minimizes the chances for misunderstanding.

Transparency

Being up front about the reasons behind a policy change goes a long way toward garnering acceptance (or at least understanding) from staff. Financial transparency is important. This doesn't have to mean sharing open-book accounts, but some level of understanding in basic financial concepts helps to make decisions clearer and more relatable. Benefits such as free post-work beers can be manageable expenses with a small staff yet become unsustainable when the headcount doubles or triples as the brewery grows. Everyone can relate to income being balanced by expenses, but the idea of "cost of goods sold" is rarely mentioned on the brewery floor and increases in raw material costs are often invisible to staff. Being open about brewery financials helps staff realize how brewery issues are interrelated, rather than viewing decisions simply as something being taken away.

Cohesion

Change is particularly difficult when leaders and managers aren't all on the same page. Leaders should be free to present their opinions during planning: their subject matter expertise is part of what makes them leaders. Once a decision is made, however, success comes from executing on that plan. When leadership undermines a policy change, the implementation will struggle.

or "pending," but even these simple acknowledgments help to enforce accountability across the team. And when an action item isn't completed by the deadline, leaders can rally to distribute more resources as needed, explain to line staff what is happening (and why), and address performance in real time rather than allowing problems to rumble on in the background.

Posting key performance indicator (KPI) boards are a powerful method for tracking follow-through. These posterboards will contain a selection of KPIs that everyone can view and see the trends in performance. Options include safety incidents (e.g., recordable events and near-misses per month/quarter), quality holds (listed by reason per month), and efficiency metrics (production and/or sustainability). Seeing actual trendlines that affect the overall health of the brewery helps provide context for why certain activities or operations are priorities and why others may not (or no longer) receive the same emphasis.

DELIVERING ENGAGEMENT

It might be said that workplace culture is defined by what happens when management isn't around. What people experience in the brewery on a daily basis is more important than what you say. A resilient organizational culture is built through consistent execution, and this requires that those at the top do their part as much as the line staff. Operators cannot be expected to meet a standard if leadership and management don't provide the necessary tools and resources.

Simplify the Process

Tasks should never be more complicated than they need to be. John Mallett always imparted to me a good rule of thumb: you should strive to engineer systems such that the easiest way to complete a task is also the right way. It doesn't matter whether the system involves how equipment is assembled, how

a procedure is structured, or how information is captured, people inevitably get tired or distracted and corners get cut. A procedure with numerous shortcuts is a poorly designed procedure that invites mistakes. When a task can be reduced to its essential steps, the chance for errors decreases.

How do you control for this? One way is to listen to what your staff is telling you. The areas that are causing frustration or losses are obvious examples. More often than not, there is a mechanical or procedural issue that can be clarified. Note that this approach doesn't mean that tasks can't be complex. Packaging lines, for example, involve mechanically complicated systems. Simplification in the packaging line involves making sure that valves, controls, and other components are clearly labeled, procedures are broken up into clearly defined tasks, and the workspace is organized to minimize clutter and make an operator's workflow simpler.

Sometimes communication isn't verbal. Brewery staff are an inventive lot and find ways to solve problems. Sometimes those are useful hacks, but others fall into the "broomstick" category (Jim Helmke, pers. comm.). Broomsticks are items used to fix the symptoms of a problem without actually fixing the problem. These can include actual broomsticks used to trigger a malfunctioning sensor, a screwdriver used to bypass a safety switch, or a chair next to a storage rack substituting for a proper ladder. Work toward solving the root causes of operator frustration rather than adding broomsticks.

Another common indicator of complexity involves process logs. Brewery logs have a way of becoming set in stone as the master copy gets photocopied batch after batch, even if the actual steps they are supposed to memorialize have long moved on from the original format. The bane of a quality manager's existence is a stack of process logs that have numerous blank spaces because "that field doesn't apply anymore." This is a recipe for important information not being recorded because blank space has been normalized.

QUALITY AS CULTURE

For me, quality starts with paperwork. Unfortunately, people avoid that step because folks don't want to look like a chair-sitter, but without well-defined specifications and procedures, you're going to struggle. I'm a paperwork guy, which can frustrate people. So it's on me to explain why the paper matters. We have to convince people that the quality steps in a procedure aren't extra work: they are the work. To build that into the culture of the brewery, I take a couple of approaches.

Be honest about how long things take

It's essential to pay attention to how you schedule work. If multitasking becomes a regular expectation, then it's a sign to me that I'm overscheduling my people. They have to have time to focus on go/no-go tasks. We try to build a full hour of loose time into everyone's workday, outside of lunch and regular breaks. I want my people to have the time to document their work, conduct the quality checks, and take care of business. It's an idea I pulled from observing a group of union carpenters: they finished each day by cleaning up their workspace and performing maintenance on their tools, which was as much a part of the job as swinging a hammer. We take the same approach and build in time accordingly. We make a point of listing the time requirements for tasks in the SOPs themselves so that people can organize their day, and I have the operators themselves work out those time requirements. I have a good idea of what's needed, but they're the ones doing it. Allotting realistic time frames helps us to avoid burning people out.

Training

Effective training requires setting clear procedures and allocating time. Start with laying the groundwork by creating procedures and continue with devoting enough time to training. Training is inefficient if it's only done through on-the-job work, especially at small breweries. Some tasks just don't happen often enough at small scales to build muscle memory. But a well-written procedure goes a long way toward mitigating this problem. Procedures can be read and reviewed and practiced in your head, so that when you have the chance to actually do the actual physical task, you're better prepared.

Because of the time commitment, we schedule training almost like classroom time. You have to budget for it. The result is worth the effort. Also be willing to overexplain the "why" of each task. Repetition matters. New staff

don't know what they don't know: you have to help them see the big picture, otherwise they'll never understand a task well enough to troubleshoot when things go wrong. Adversity is our best trainer. Our job is to prepare them for the problems that will inevitably happen.

Accountability

I'm a huge believer in documenting our work. Every fermentation log starts with the cleaning and sanitation records, and we document every stage of the brewing process. It's a lot of paper, but establishing a record matters when a problem happens. Otherwise you're guessing. We also make it practice of reviewing work logs. It isn't a gotcha situation to catch people, it's a recognition that we have to inspect what you expect. This allows us the opportunity to detect drifts in performance (whether in the process or the operator) before they settle into habits.

Brewery work gets busy, so regularly scanning through brewhouse or packaging logs helps me to understand where pressure points are. If something is getting skipped over, I may need to make adjustments to the SOP or schedule to make sure that quality checks aren't the item that gets skipped.

Positive reinforcement

Recognizing good performance is incredibly important. I have to value what I want my staff to value. Saying so publicly makes a difference. When people start to care, they take pride in hitting their brewhouse gravities or DO checks. And it means a lot to staff when a visiting brewer is impressed by what they see in our workspace. Being told that your place looks like it's wired tight just feels good. You may see the flaws, but public recognition gets people to invest in keeping the place dialed in. People step up when the results are noticed and acknowledged.

—Larry Horwitz
Head of Brewing, Ten20 Craft Brewing

Measure Twice, Cut Once

Breweries are busy spaces, and you may be tempted to make changes on the fly. Pressing equipment or procedures into service without thinking through how it will affect operations has safety and quality implications, but it also has an impact on your staff. They are the ones who end up having to deal with a kludgy implementation. The expectations for service or quality won't diminish in this situation; rather, employees will figure out ways to deal with it. The effects might be temporary, but the danger is when perceived values start to shift away from your goals. Remember, every workplace has an organizational culture but it may not be the one you want.

The solution to this potential problem is to invest time in advance planning wherever and whenever possible. Having spare parts on hand is one example of advance planning, but so is preparing for personnel changes through cross-training employees. Shifting a person with the necessary skills into a role temporarily will have a very different outcome than tossing an untrained person into the deep end and hoping for the best until a new hire can be made.

Talking through SOP changes with line operators before rollout should be considered the bare minimum, but there are also benefits to running changes past others in the brewery. Many breweries don't have a dedicated maintenance team, so getting advice from a mechanically inclined employee can catch expensive installation issues in advance. The employee's skill set is what matters, not whether they're on the production or taproom side.

Be Responsive

Trust is gained in drips but lost in buckets. Leadership can't address situations they don't know about—without trust, there are conversations that simply won't happen. Procedures can be modified, equipment can be moved, but a reputation for not valuing employees is hard to recover from. It sets a tone that affects both current and future staff members, even ones who are hired long after a situation was resolved.

For values to be more than aspirational, your brewery has to ensure that they are applied consistently. This is a simple lesson to learn, but many breweries learn it the hard way. What distinguishes an effective leadership team is its reaction to problems and how it adjusts operations to prevent a recurrence. It is important to point out that having a relevant policy or training program doesn't eliminate problems. Those policies and programs are preventive, but culture is about lived experience.

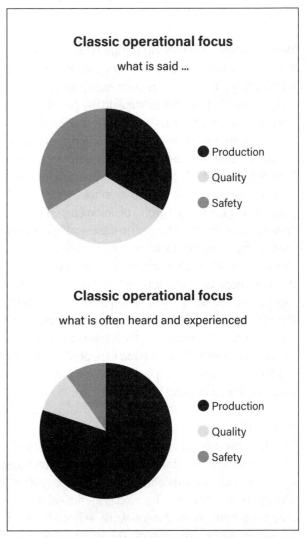

Figure 6.4. What gets said during a meeting often doesn't survive the transition to the actual working environment. Messages can be changed overtly or inadvertently, but the net effect is that staff may take away a very different set of expectations than what you intended. Pay attention to what is put into practice, not just the meeting notes.

WORKING TO ENSURE STAFF WELL-BEING

Fostering engagement is essential to developing a healthy work culture. Having said that, organizations can appear to be healthy at first glance but have serious issues once you look deeper. The craft brewing sector is very good at creating an image and public persona

CULTURE AS AN ORGANIZATIONAL EFFORT

of celebrating creativity, iconoclasts, and collegiality. A phrase often used in brewing circles is that craft brewing is 99 percent asshole-free. This simply isn't true and never has been. Perhaps more accurately, the lived experience of this depends on who you are in the industry and the corresponding treatment you receive from peers. The claim rings true for the experience of many, no question. For many others who have tried to establish a brewing career, the industry is filled with obstacles, gatekeepers, and antagonism.

Acknowledging this is a start, but the real work involves working to establish and support organizational cultures within breweries that address these factors. This partly involves structural work, such as how you hire and review staff. But culture is deeply rooted in team dynamics, which can be supportive and welcoming or cliquish and closed off. How these work environments form involves the kinds of individual behaviors that are rewarded by teams versus rejected.

RESPONDING TO HARASSMENT, DISCRIMINATION, AND VIOLENCE

The presence of harassing, discriminatory, and violent behaviors within the brewing industry cannot and should not be ignored. It has pushed out too many from the industry and discouraged others from joining in the first place. The reality of sexual assaults and harassment (SAH) in particular is something the community must face head on. It's important to recognize that these issues aren't isolated to brewery staff interactions. Employee-customer and employee-vendor interactions are equally vulnerable to abusive behavior. To paraphrase Dr. J Jackson-Beckham, this is not a "bad actor" issue: removing an individual without changing the cultural conditions leaves the door open to for future bad actors to thrive in the same environment.[*]

The first step in shaping cultural conditions involves setting up a code of conduct that addresses these issues. From there, you have to take direct steps toward confronting precursor behaviors. These precursor behaviors might be overt, such as demeaning jokes and sexual innuendo. Precursor behaviors can take other forms, like not taking training sessions on discrimination and SAH seriously: many see these trainings as a burden rather than a reflection of what their peers may be facing in the workplace.

Leaders have an obligation to respond to discriminatory behavior, whether it is a "joke" or obvious bullying behavior. There is no requirement for a formal complaint to be made in order for you to intervene. In fact, not responding makes it even less likely that employees will feel comfortable lodging a complaint. Leadership has to take an active role, because looking the other way will most certainly shape workplace culture, just not in the direction you want.

Developing a complaints procedure is equally important. While permissive behaviors are often out in the open, incidents of abuse or harassment will frequently occur away from the public eye. Employees must have a way to report issues that will lead to action.

A more subtle sign of harassment or discrimination is employees who begin withdrawing from the wider team, socially or within the brewery. These are indications that more investigation is needed. Touching base with employees who seem withdrawn is important. It may be that they have stressors outside of the brewery that are occupying their mind, but the reason may be deeper problems within the brewery.

[*]   J. Nikol Jackson-Beckham, "The Unthinkable Has Happened: Finding Your Way After Harassment, Discrimination, or Abuse Has Changed Everything" (PowerPoint/Keynote presentation, Craft Brewers Conference, Denver, CO, September, 2021, https://www.brewersassociation.org/seminars/the-unthinkable-has-happened-finding-your-way-after-harassment-discrimination-or-abuse-has-changed-everything/).

Harassment

Often categorized as verbal or physical abuse, harassment is a much broader set of behaviors. Whether called teasing, hazing, horseplay, or "just jokes," these are differences in degree, not kind. What these behaviors have in common is that certain people or groups are treated as an "other" or as not genuinely belonging to the team. These actions may not be intentional, but intent isn't the metric that matters—how they are received is what affects the team. People who feel excluded from the group, however unintentionally, will pull back and withdraw. This outcome is not only ethically wrong, it may have legal implications. The point is that a team is strongest when it includes all the talents and skills available to it, regardless of who brings them to the table.

INVESTIGATING HARASSMENT, DISCRIMINATION, AND VIOLENCE

Properly handling an investigation has complexities that are outside the scope of this book, but there are best practice guidelines, starting with taking reports seriously. Don't look away because it is difficult or uncomfortable.

- **Leaders have an obligation to follow up on information about these issues.**
  - Even when there is a desire for a conversation to be "off the record," the brewery has to respond.
  - There is no requirement for complaints to be formally reported: if you're aware of an issue, you must investigate.
- **Investigations need to be prompt, thorough, and impartial.**
  - The impartiality component is the hardest for small organizations; bringing in a third party may be required.
- **Investigations should look at three core areas:**
  - People – Interview the complainant, respondent, and relevant witnesses
    - Don't base credibility on physical demeanor: stress is real and affects how people respond. Focus on the facts, not the delivery.
  - Places – Assess the space(s) where the alleged behavior took place
    - Are there security cameras or places where potential witnesses could have been?
  - Things – Review any electronic media (particularly emails, text messages, instant/direct messages, and social media comments), security camera footage, and other forms of establishing location and time frames, such as time cards/punches.
- **Completing investigations**
  - The standard is a preponderance of evidence: is it more likely than not that the behavior took place?
  - Document the investigation and the conclusion
    - Write notes as you go
    - The summary should be clear, fact-based, and concise
- **Closure**
  - Be as transparent as possible—trust is essential
    - With cases involving sexual abuse, there are privacy limits on what can and should be shared; seek legal counsel as needed.
  - Acknowledge the closure with the participants, including witnesses—don't leave people hanging.

Further information can be found through the Resource Hub on the Brewers Association website (https://www.brewersassociation.org/resource-hub/dei/), particularly a 2019 Craft Brewers Conference seminar called "Ignorance is Not Bliss: Workplace Investigation Basics."

Historically, several groups have borne the brunt of workplace harassment in the brewing industry. Many such individuals have been members of the craft brewing movement for decades, not to mention being part of brewing history for centuries before that. While there have been some recent improvements with respect to gender and racial equality and increased recognition of the LBGTQ+ community, the day-to-day working environment for many in the craft brewing industry remains deeply, deeply problematic, no matter how many high-profile trailblazers we see. The brewing industry has the opportunity to be accepting of all members of the community but, sadly, it remains a reflection of society as a whole. Women in the industry continue to be treated as novel and routinely have their experience and knowledge overlooked or dismissed. Meanwhile, targeting your marketing to specific events like celebrating Pride or observing Juneteenth aren't the same as addressing how entire communities are treated on a daily basis.

Brewery leaders and managers have a responsibility to support the entire staff, and this includes monitoring for harassment, whether it is outright hostility or "just a joke" that crosses a line. Note that these lines aren't drawn by or for those with authority: they exist to protect those who feel excluded. Many of the concepts discussed in earlier chapters can be brought to bear on this:

- Selection of employees based on job-specific aptitude, not preconceptions of "cultural fit"
- Thorough training that establishes a common knowledge base and emphasizes organizational values
- Communicating regularly with your teams. If your employees don't trust you, you'll be blind to their concerns.

Substance Abuse

Working within the brewing industry and the connected hospitality sector carries risks associated with substance abuse. Workers have immediate access to alcohol and ready access to other materials. Factor in the odd hours and considerable stress involved, and it adds up to many opportunities for the use of intoxicating substances to get out of control.

The warning signs can include physical, mental, and behavioral changes. Simply from an ethical standpoint, supporting employees struggling with substance abuse is important: you should always strive to take care of your people. Best practices for providing this support include (Haslam 2022):

- offering support rather than blame,
- providing empathy and understanding, and
- presenting resources and options, rather than demands.

While sensory work in the brewing industry often involves consuming beer, this is not a requirement. Expecting alcohol consumption as part of the job is an unnecessary complication for staff seeking to maintain sobriety. Training other members of the staff to be sensory panelists is an immediate work accommodation and also serves as professional development for the rest of the team.

Offering access to resources such as employee assistance programs (EAPs) can provide significant help with corollary issues often associated with substance use and other stressors, such as difficult financial situations, legal complications, or relationship problems. All of these can contribute to a vicious cycle that accelerates substance abuse.

Avoiding Burnout

The brewing industry has a perception problem: both inside and outside of the brewery walls, there is a view that brewery work is a never-ending party, fast-paced and just generally awesome. This is true in part, but it comes with a cost. In real life, every aspect of a brewery environment involves super-hard work, both physical and mental. This is true in production, taproom operations, and sales. The specific tasks are different, but the effect of that intensity takes a toll on everyone.

Small breweries are particularly vulnerable to this effect because scaling and growth pose a massive challenge. There often isn't enough money to increase staffing, so duties overlap. Filling in gaps becomes expected and then set in stone. Extended hours become extensive and then excessive. This has always been a challenge for small businesses, but the craft brewing sector saw itself as an exception for a long time. That perception is being peeled apart now. The COVID-19 pandemic has been an accelerant, but the kindling was always there.

PLANNING TO PREVENT BURNOUT

When researching burnout, I interviewed Katie Muggli about putting systems in place to prevent burnout. Katie is the founder and director of Infinite Ingredients. She outlines three areas where leadership has to deliver:
1. Providing access to tangible resources (e.g., paid time off, employee assistance programs)
2. Removing barriers to utilizing these resources
3. Making sure that good intentions have deliberate and consistent follow-through

From an employee perspective, the follow-through is the most important aspect. Muggli points out why this is the case: "There is a vast chasm between what owners and senior leaders can see as the reality in the brewery and what the day-to-day staff experiences. This cognitive dissonance drives conflict and wastes an enormous amount of potential."

Things to look out for in employee behavior that may indicate burnout:
- Reduced performance and productivity—watch out for your high performers, are they running out of steam? Why?

- Absenteeism—if someone is calling in frequently, or is out sick, or is out sick consistently from being hungover, that can be a huge red flag

- An increasingly cynical outlook on work, which can lead to quickness to anger and emotional numbness and apathy when dealing with coworkers, guests, and accounts

Things for leadership/owners/managers to consider that can help create healthier and more psychologically safe work environments:
- Self-awareness: Know your strengths and weaknesses. Should you be leading a team? Should you be managing? This is a tough question, but is most certainly one worth asking yourself, because if you're burning out as a manager, leader, or owner it's likely that if your team is following your example, they're probably feeling it too.

- Take accountability for burnout among your teams and across your organization. Is there one team that is burned out, but another that is thriving? Why is that? Don't be afraid to take an honest and hard look at how your own strengths and weaknesses inform this.

- Evaluate workloads: Are they realistic? Are they sustainable?

- Have staffing plans: At what point do you need to hire additional people? This goes hand in hand with evaluating workloads—people can go at 150% and thrive and build and do well ... for a while.

  - When is help being called in? Is there even a plan to bring in help? If you think you can't afford to make another hire and your staffing plan is to burnout your best and brightest, recall that 33% turnover mark on a person's salary and ask yourself if you can afford that cost continually.
  - Your best and brightest will also take their institutional knowledge out the door with them. As a startup or newer company, that institutional knowledge is incredibly important and valuable.

- Create clear working hours and stick to them to avoid the "always-on" expectation. Are you always on because you are an owner? That's a you problem—do not expect your employees to model your behavior.

    - If an employee is salaried, make clear designations for "on" hours and stick to them. Don't send a text or call at 9 p.m. with something that can wait until morning.
    - If you have an employee calling in outside of their "on" hours, check in with them as to why they are working so late. What resources can you provide for them? What can you take off their plate?

- A clear designation of roles and responsibilities helps employees understand what is and is not in their purview. What are they responsible for? If things are ambiguous, you can wind up with significant stressors within teams and across the organization that are completely avoidable.

- Accountability across the organization is really important.
    - The biggest takeaway here is that accountability must stretch across the whole organization— managers, leaders, and owners should not be immune to accountability for mistakes. It will be extremely fatiguing for employees to see that a different set of rules applies to them versus their coworkers.
    - If your brewery truly works as a team, you will take full responsibility for your actions and impact on the team, and have the same, if not higher, standards that apply to those in managerial positions, leadership roles, and owners.

- Set a clear time-off policy: offering an unlimited time-off policy to the full-time/salaried staff sounds incredibly generous, but if roles and responsibilities aren't clearly designated, it can be really difficult, if not impossible, for individuals to take time off. Worse yet, this policy can make people feel guilty about taking time off for fear of not wanting to be seen as abusing it; and it can become something that is easily weaponized as a show of dedication in not taking it.

    - If you have or would like to institute a unlimited time-off policy, don't leave it undefined. Monitor how it is used, and check in with employees who aren't utilizing their time off. Understanding why they aren't using it may point to some unmet need or issue that should be addressed by clarifying roles, offering support, and or improving company culture.

- Develop and promote job resources that cover training, pathways for learning, and professional development.

    - Without these resources, you may have someone experiencing burnout, rather than a fully engaged employee who is supported and able to deliver their best work for the company.
    - If you have clear opportunities and pathways for people, they will likely be more engaged knowing that there is not only a plan for moving forward, but opportunities for investment in their professional growth and development. Engagement helps lead to loyalty and longevity in tenure.

- Provide a safe work environment: this is super important for both physical and psychological safety.
    - We talk a great deal in the brewing industry about physical safety, but psychological safety is a huge component in creating a safe work environment.
    - Providing a work environment that is psychologically safe means you have a workplace where employees can voice concerns, make mistakes, and voice new ideas without fear of being punished or humiliated.

7
EVOLVING YOUR BREWERY'S CULTURE

In 2007, there were roughly 1,400 active brewing licenses in the United States. By 2015, that number had grown to 4,000.[1] This was the second time the American brewing industry had had so many members: the first time was in 1870 (Holle et al. 2012, 9). At that time, the first installation of commercial refrigeration in a brewery wouldn't happen until three years later, in Germany, and the now ubiquitous brewhouse whirlpool wouldn't be developed for another 90 years (Mosher 2009, 15; Klimovitz 2012).

The fundamental biochemistry of brewing hasn't changed much since 1870, but almost every other aspect of the brewing landscape has. The differences are significant even when comparing the first wave of homebrewers and entrepreneurs who transformed their hobby into a professional career in the early 1970s and 80s with the current American craft beer scene.

Regardless of annual barrelage or your chosen business model, every brewery has to ask itself, "What do we bring to the market, and how do we bring experience into existence?" The counterpoint is what consumers ask themselves with every purchase: "Why should I spend my disposable income on your beer rather than with your competitors?" The corresponding operational component involves working out how to meet and exceed those consumer expectations and do it in a way that is sustainable over the long term. That is the challenge if you are to last in an increasingly competitive market.

Meeting these challenges requires something that was discussed all the way back in the introduction: you have to invest in your people. Physical infrastructure can be added and upgraded, but it is your employee base that will drive success. Note that this is not a function of scale—every brewery is faced with having to establish a culture that brings out the best in its teams. Resources will always be finite, so establishing priorities and a commitment to accountability remains critical. It's important to recognize, however, that these priorities will change over time as conditions change. Items such as safety, morale, and quality will remain on the list, but the relative rankings will shift as situations warrant.

---

[1] "Brewery Production," Stats and Data, Brewers Association, accessed October 17, 2022, https://www.brewersassociation.org/statistics-and-data/brewery-production-data/.

WORKPLACE CULTURES EXIST TO MEET THE MOMENT

Just as your business plan has to adapt to change, your workplace culture also has to be capable of evolving to match the challenges that arise. Some of these will be a natural part of the normal growth of a brewery, while others will present external obstacles that affect the arc of operations (fig. 7.1). As a brewery grows and matures over time, it has to plan for how the core values and attributes that made it successful are retained. At the same time, a brewery needs to be prepared to let go of aspects that negatively affect the organization.

The early days of a brewery can be an exhausting but exhilarating experience. The staff of a brewery when it first opens tend to bring a high degree of emotional investment to the project: these employees are in on the ground floor of a new venture and can operate with more independence than they would have in an established brewery. Over time, however, the frenetic pace of the launch phase will fade and, whether through growth or turnover, new faces will begin to appear in the brewery. Professionalism and paychecks will become more important than being part of something brand-new.

This is a natural sequence of events, so the challenge is to maintain within your staff the same sense of urgency, desire, and passion for the job that got the brewery through its opening. The demands of operations and expectations of customers don't care whether an employee has been on the job since Day One or is only in their first week: either way, the job needs to be done correctly. This is why the previous chapters emphasize establishing consistent structures to guide organizational culture. For new employees in an established business, connecting to the brewery's past and appreciating its legacy is important so they can see themselves as part of an ongoing effort. These employees can't be part of the past but they can shape the future. Guiding them to this point is essential for the long-term engagement that drives a successful operation.

COMMUNITY ENGAGEMENT

Bent Paddle Brewery runs a community engagement program called "Paddle It Forward" that focuses on projects in the local community and the broader North Shore of Minnesota. It is difficult to draw brewery personnel into common projects like trail maintenance or park clean-ups. The projects are on the weekend, and even a community project can feel like extra work after they've been in the brewery all week. Forced volunteering isn't volunteering, so Bent Paddle looks for other avenues that engage staff and stay true to the brewery's community mission. Some of the most popular and successful have been:

- encouraging staff to select non-profits for the brewery to engage with, either through donating time, money, or visibility;
- providing $100 in matching funds annually for employee donations to the charities of their choice.

Both of these options allow employees to connect the brewery's community mission with their own passions and interests. That sense of connection and participation makes a difference.

Laura Mullen
Vice President, Outreach and Events,
Bent Paddle Brewery

Inception	Launch	Consolidation	Stability	Relevance
Clear vision; business plan; establishing core leadership	Site build-out & equipment installation; hiring & training staff; developing the consumer-facing image; sticking the landing for those first few months	Review the launch phase to determine what worked and what didn't; getting a handle on process & policy; focus on internal execution	Recognize what the consumer wants and delivering those beers and experiences consistently; monitor internal habits, but focus on external execution	Monitor market trends; listen to consumer impressions of your brand; decide whether your original vision is working: if yes, keep at it, if not, look for an authentic pivot

Figure 7.1. Managing the Stages of Brewery Growth. A brewery goes through multiple phases as it develops, each with its own challenges. Thinking through what is coming next helps to prepare the organization for change.

Brewery tasks can become monotonous when performing the same routines over and over. These repetitive tasks are what generate cash flow, but breaking up the monotony and keeping teams mentally fresh and engaged helps ensure long-term stability. There are several ways to accomplish this, many of which we've already covered in this book. Even if you have already implemented some of these programs and policies, you should always be looking at them through the lens of continually adjusting and adapting to changing environments. You can help prepare your staff for change by providing them with challenges and opportunities.

Cross-Training and Rotations

As discussed in chapter 3, cross-training adds to the strength of the organization by deepening the reservoir of critical skills within teams and improving their flexibility. Even when skills are already broadly distributed through the staff, tasks can be concentrated by shift schedules or within a department. For example, yeast handling expertise can be concentrated within a set of employees because of how they're scheduled. If there is turnover or a shift changes, it can lead to a skills gap. Other members of the team may understand how to perform the tasks, but skills degrade when they aren't practiced routinely.

Setting up job rotations helps keep skills and muscle memory fresh. Moving employees through various brewery functions also helps avoid silos forming between teams. This is particularly important when integrating new employees. Studies show that it can take some people up to a year to fully integrate new skills and become confident in their tasks. Blending new and experienced staff helps to reduce the learning curve.

Rotating through teams is exceptionally useful for aspiring leaders and managers. Developing a deep and highly specialized understanding of a particular area is one way to advance, but managers in particular benefit from having a broad understanding of the entire brewery. Having to work with a variety of teams also places people in a situation where they will be exposed to different challenges. Adapting to challenges is the definition of problem-solving, which is the most valuable skill in a brewery.

Small breweries often do staff rotation by default because having a small staff forces everyone to wear a variety of hats, but small breweries still need to guard against being vulnerable to turnover. When one person does a specific task almost every time, skills in other tasks will atrophy.

An expanding brewery has to engage in rotational exposure in order to develop leaders and broaden skills through the entire team. Expecting someone to take the lead on a major new initiative while also expecting them to continue performing their original tasks may be workable in the short term, but when it becomes the new normal, it is a recipe for burnout (we discussed burnout in the previous chapter, see p. 97).

Every manager of a shift rotation schedule has to decide what the frequency of the rotations will be. Durations lasting one to two weeks can wreak havoc on sleep schedules, which is a hazard considering the range of dangers present in a brewery. Quarterly rotations offer considerable stability for staff members, but this can come at the cost of relationships and life outside the brewery. Rotation schedules in the four- to six-week range offer a combination of consistency, flexibility, and sufficient time to adapt sleep schedules (table 7.1).

BENEFITS OF CROSS-TRAINING AND JOB ROTATION

- Skill building
- Flexibility in staffing
- Keep skills current
- Improve communication
- Build bridges between departments
- Improve quality assurance

Creative Outlets

One of the joys of homebrewing is experimentation, self-expression, and brewing whatever sounds interesting to you at a given moment in time. Brewing professionally is an exercise in managing market capture: the consumers have an outsized effect on what will be the next brew on the schedule. Even in small breweries with the freedom to churn through new recipes, creative control usually isn't open to all. Most brewery work involves executing someone else's vision, not expressing your own. Encouraging creativity and providing outlets has a direct impact on engagement. Done smartly, these efforts also don't need to be resource intensive. You just need to be clever about it.

Table 7.1 **Example of a shift rotation schedule.**

By rotating through different tasks, operators maintain proficiency in all aspects of the position.

BLOCK	TIME (sample)	DUTIES
OPEN	05:00–13:30	Brewhouse and cellar operators (paired for safety)
MID - Support	09:00–17:30	Assists throughout the brewery, covering lunches, breaks, and the gap between opening and closing shifts
CLOSE	15:00–22:30	Brewhouse and cellar operators (paired for safety)

ROTATION BLOCK	OPEN	MID	CLOSE
1	Brewhouse		
2		Support	
3			Cellar
4			Brewhouse
5		Support	
6	Cellar		
1 (Restart the cycle)	Brewhouse		

CORE BRANDS PAY THE BILLS, PILOT BEERS SATISFY THE CREATIVE ITCH

Part of the excitement around brewing is coming up with new beers. In small operations, a regular rotation of fresh recipes is the name of the game, but the reality of brewing is that new recipes don't happen every day. More often, a handful of beers will become core brands due to consistent consumer demand. Repeat customers lead to steady cash flow, so those brands stay in rotation and get brewed regularly, sometimes to the exclusion of new recipe ideas.

Not everyone will be part of the process when new beers are being developed, however. People will still look for creative outlets to express themselves, so try to provide an avenue for this. Even the smallest brewery can bring in a homebrewing setup and give employees an opportunity to develop new recipes and ideas. Creative outlets like this have been successfully duplicated at breweries of all sizes.

Collaborations

"Collabs" have been a feature of the craft brewing scene for over a decade, providing an opportunity for brewers to engage with peers from other breweries. Some collaborations attempt to blend the particular expertise of each participant into a combination that exemplifies the best of both breweries. The Sierra Nevada Beer Camp series was an excellent example of this.

Other collaborations are an opportunity to experiment with an ingredient or technique that is novel to both breweries. Combining expertise and skills can help to navigate a new process. Regardless of how the recipe is developed, these events are an excellent way for brewers to get out of their comfort zone and see new ways of performing tasks.

Community Engagement

Collaborations don't have to be limited to other breweries. Partnering with local organizations to develop a new beer is an opportunity for more than marketing exposure or charitable works. These beers offer a canvas to create something that would be outside the brewery's normal wheelhouse.

A specific version of this idea involves partnerships with local homebrew groups through some variation of the pro-am concept. Having a competition or contest to select a recipe to be made on the brewery's system is an excellent way to further outreach to the local brewing community.

Innovation Through Professional Development

A successful program conducted by SanTan Brewery in Arizona involves a 2-barrel system. Employees submit a concept proposal and recipe, which are reviewed by the wider team. The point isn't to gatekeep ideas; rather, the goal is to help teach shift brewers how to develop workable recipes that have a business case behind them. In addition to creativity, this process doubles as professional development, helping brewers look at the bigger picture of the brewery as a business. There are three basic questions embedded in the proposal: (1) What are you trying to accomplish, (2) How would it fit into the draught board, and (3) Does the beer make financial sense? Recipes coming through this program can be as off-the-wall as the brewers want, but going through the exercise of making the case for a beer concept is important for developing a career in the industry.

As part of the program, brewers are welcome to run a full mash-lauter cycle, but the 2-barrel system is also tied into the main 50-barrel brewhouse. This allows staff to draw off any of the regular production wort streams and then manipulate the wort as their recipe requires. Pulling from existing wort streams helps reduce the time commitment, which reduces a significant barrier—having permission to do something cool isn't the same as having time available to do it. The handful of sixtel kegs produced will go on tap at the taproom. This is exciting for staff at a personal and professional level, and can even lead to the recipe being scaled up to SanTan's 15-barrel system or guiding the development of other brand concepts.

Team-Building

Pilot systems offer a way to bring people on your staff together. As breweries grow and evolve, some groups who are deeply tied to your brewery become disconnected from the actual process. In particular, taproom and sales staff are the de facto public faces of the brewery, but most have little to no experience with how beer is actually made.

Developing employees' connection with the actual beer-making process helps them both understand your beers and engage more effectively with customers. It's hard to duplicate the passion that comes from seeing something you were a part of being ordered by a customer. Providing opportunities for non-brewing staff to internally collaborate on a pilot batch of something that will be served in your taproom is an excellent way to both educate staff and provide a teambuilding opportunity that bridges gaps between teams.

Creativity isn't limited to recipes. Problem-solving in the brewery can be treated as a creative outlet. Providing resources to tackle immediate headaches or research future challenges is incredibly valuable. Allowing staff members to explore their professional interests and nurture their passions will pay dividends across the entire team. Conferences or internal projects both provide opportunities along these lines.

Matching a company goal, such as establishing a sensory program, to an employee or team interested in developing the topic helps everyone involved: the brewery gains new functionality while investing in its most important resource. By the same token, assigning an employee a handful of conference sessions specific to a particular brewery need emphasizes the team aspect of professional development; meanwhile, giving the employee free rein to plan the rest of their conference schedule allows them the freedom to explore their own interests.

Another option is to establish a budget category for funding professional education that has applicability to the brewery. This could be coursework on project management or advanced spreadsheet methods at a community college, a CPR/AED class, or reimbursing staff for professional certification exam fees. The financial resources of the individual brewery will govern the size of this pool of money, but awards can be capped at a fixed amount per year and require a passing grade to encourage accountability.

Providing these opportunities adds value to the brewery, so it is important to devote the necessary resources for successful implementation. Sending an employee to a seminar on sensory panels and then not providing the time, money, and attention necessary to incorporate those lessons into the brewery is a waste for everyone. There will be upfront costs, but the benefits will come over time.

Those benefits should also be shared with staff: adding new responsibilities without compensating that work will take a toll on team morale.

EVOLUTION: LOOKING TOWARD THE FUTURE

The brewing industry isn't a static environment. Changing retail environments, consumer preferences, beer styles, and supply chain pressures all demand that breweries be adaptable and prepared for change. Nor is beer alone in the alcoholic beverage sector: wine and distilled spirits remain significant competition for discretionary dollars, and CBD- and THC-infused beverages have begun to appear in the market.

The organizational challenge we need to address is that market trends and conditions move quickly, while changing culture takes time. Resilient cultures are capable of being nimble and quick to adapt, but this is because they are already dialed in. Dysfunctional organizations may look like they are changing rapidly from the outside, but these are gains built on sand. Stability and effectiveness during a pivot come from putting in the work in advance to understand their needs and plan accordingly.

CONFERENCES AND PROFESSIONAL DEVELOPMENT OPPORTUNITIES

Bent Paddle Brewery sees conferences as an opportunity for rewarding staff, providing professional development, and furthering business relationships. Conferences are expensive commitments, so the brewery starts by looking at its budget: how many people can it afford to send to a specific location? From there, it considers who has attended in the past and then works up a list of who will attend. Ideally, there is a mix of owners, senior staff, and line staff from various parts of the brewery. Connecting as a team at a conference is important: organizing team dinners helps break down barriers and create chances for small group conversations.

At the individual level, conference attendance is a reward for some, recognition for prior work, a chance to visit a new location and connect with peers from other breweries. Others are tasked with looking forward by attending specific presentations to bring information back to the brewery. These staff are expected to relay that knowledge to the brewery as a whole, either through projects or recaps to coworkers. A key task for staff involved in vendor relationships is making time to talk with every supplier they do business with, whether that is having dinner, drinks, or simply chatting during the trade show.

Selecting a conference and who will attend is always a reflection of what we feel the brewery needs at the time. We try to match the individual opportunity to a brewery challenge. This gives us some structure to use when making (and when necessary, explaining) conference decisions. Some staff members have to attend conferences because it's part of their job, but it is important for us to bring other employees as well. Our staff are the future of Bent Paddle, so it just comes down to making the best use of our resources every year.

Laura Mullen
Vice President, Outreach and Events, Bent Paddle Brewery

Periodic Program Reviews: Looking in the Mirror

All breweries change over time, and so do their needs and capabilities. Operationally, performance audits investigate whether tasks are being performed correctly. Safety audits, SOP spot-checks, and KPI reviews are all examples of measuring items to better manage them.

With organizational culture, you also want to know whether the tools and programs in current use are adequate to the challenges being faced. If yesterday's programs do not address today's conditions, performance will suffer. Overlooking this step is the root of every "but we've always down it this way" argument, and it is entirely avoidable. This problem becomes amplified when you begin to plan for growth without first spending enough time working through the personnel and skill requirements.

Periodically reviewing the brewery's programs and policies is invaluable from the standpoint of an evolving culture. As the adage says, you can't manage what you don't measure. When performing a policy and programs review, there is a series of questions you can ask to gauge whether the programs you developed based on the building blocks laid down in the first four chapters are still working as intended and will be suited for future plans.

Employee Feedback

Another valuable initiative to ensure workplace culture evolves is soliciting feedback from staff. This is distinct from the submission of employee ideas via conversations or some form of suggestion box. Here, you want to deliberately ask questions that will give insight into how employees genuinely view the workplace and what they value versus making assumptions about what is motivating staff behavior. The reality on the brewery floor can differ dramatically from the view of management. Essentially, soliciting feedback is conducting a performance review on an entire team or organization.

Surveys provide a snapshot of a particular moment in time. Asking the same set of questions year over year gives you a window into developing trends, positive or negative, in your brewery's organizational culture. These can also be connected to objective measures like KPIs on safety, production efficiency, or quality metrics. When you consider that profit is a direct result of operational efficiency, the collective mindset of the brewery staff matters a great deal. Improvements in efficiency that come at the expense of employee morale will be short-lived.

Looking Forward: Think about the Future Now

In Chapter 1, we looked at outlining the immediate and near-term needs of the brewery so that you could draw a picture of what you're looking for in a new hire. The same exercise is needed as you come to consider future needs. What kind of teams will you need? If you're adding new teams or shifts, you'll need leadership and management support: where will they come from? Bootstrapping an entire department from scratch will either take time or cost a significant amount of money.

Opening a catering/event division or a satellite location (with or without a functioning brewery) is a sizeable investment in people and general infrastructure. Sourcing the staff who have the knowledge and experience to represent the brand at the same level as the flagship location doesn't happen overnight. The same holds true for investing in a new packaging line or expanding into new sales markets.

An effective organizational culture involves applying consistent effort to developing your own successors. Personnel who guard specific tasks and knowledge are inhibiting the growth of the organization. This is particularly true when the behavior is an attempt to be "irreplaceable." This simply isn't a productive approach. Mentoring colleagues actually increases value. Arguably, making sure no one is irreplaceable also improves quality of life for your people: if an employee can never take a vacation because they are "essential" or they will return to find their desk buried by tasks not completed in their absence, it is an exhausting approach to work that is ultimately unsustainable. Resilient, effective teams have a broad understanding of everyone's roles and duties and members can step in as needed to share the workload.

There isn't a crystal ball that will identify every developing trend that will affect your brewery, but the process of looking forward is intended to identify areas of opportunity, from which you can work toward building the flexibility that will allow the brewery to pivot when the right moment presents itself. For example, the purchase of scientific equipment often happens faster than developing the staff expected to use that equipment. If you have invested in creating a flexible, well-trained workforce then you have a significant competitive advantage. Resources such as *Quality Management* and *Quality Labs for Small Brewers* can help you plan for future laboratory requirements depending on your brewery's size

POLICY AND PROGRAMS REVIEW: QUESTIONS TO ASK

You can assess whether existing programs and policies are up-to-date and ready for future challenges by asking the following questions.

Selection (chap. 1)

- Do job postings accurately reflect the positions and desired attributes?
- Are you attracting the caliber of candidates you want?
  - If not, how are you going to address recruitment?
- Is the interview process yielding useable results?
  - Are you covering the full range of job duties?
  - Are you learning enough to differentiate candidates on those factors?
  - Is important information slipping through the cracks?

Training and Development (chaps. 2 and 3)

- Does the training pipeline deliver capable team members?
  - If not, can you identify common factors?
    - Employee performance
    - Instructor performance
    - Flaws with SOPs, e.g., being out of date, incomplete, etc.
    - Insufficient time/availability being allotted to cover assigned tasks
  - Are SOPs being reviewed and updated?
  - Are changes to SOPs being communicated to all employees affected?
- Ongoing education
  - Are managers providing enough time and other resources?
    - Safety refreshers, sensory panels, cross-training, etc.
  - Are teams empowered to request topics?
  - Do educational opportunities address brewery needs and regulatory requirements?

- Equity
  - Are opportunities available to and shared across all qualified members of the team?
    - If not, what's going on?

Performance Reviews and Management Actions (chaps. 4 and 5)

- Reviews
  - Are reviews being performed in a timely fashion?
  - Are ratings clear, consistent, and evidence-based?
- Feedback
  - Are managers requesting feedback from staff?
  - Do employees feel empowered to provide feedback?
  - Are managers following up on employee feedback and suggestions?
  - Are there alternate pathways for situations where employees may have to deliver feedback to a supervisor, manager, or owner who has a conflict of interest?
- Reporting and support (see also chapter 6)
  - Are reports of harassment being investigated and addressed?
  - Are indicators of substance abuse or other behavioral warning signs being addressed?
  - Do employees feel supported or singled out?
  - Are disciplinary actions being documented clearly and consistently applied?
    - If not, what is the plan to address this?

and sales model (Pellettieri 2015; Waldron 2020, 189–192). The Brewers Association website has further resources like *Design and Construction of Brewery Quality Labs* by the Brewers Association's Engineering Subcommittee.

Succession Planning

A best practice is to encourage leaders at every level to mentor and develop their own successors. At the senior leadership level, including ownership, breweries are well-served by spending time thinking about the succession planning process in detail. Every brewery needs to think about the long haul and develop a plan for the future.

There are two common formats for mapping out who will take over a role later down the line: the heir model and the pool model (Berkley and Kaplan 2020, 262–263). The heir model is pretty much what is sounds like: designating a specific person to slot into a role once the current occupant departs. This is also known as replacement planning. Training and advancement is specifically targeted to prepare the replacement to take over the reins.

The pool model looks past specific positions and instead focuses on the overall health of the organization. What this means in practice is that an organization concentrates its energy on having both

FACTORS THAT INFLUENCE FUTURE GROWTH

Having a realistic understanding of your own operations is essential. It is also worth looking outward and evaluating peers and competitors: what are behaviors you want to emulate, and what mistakes do you want to avoid? What follows are examples of areas you can examine to increase this self-awareness.

Owners and Senior Management
- Factors that affect multiple operational components of the brewery
  - Growth targets (supply chain, production, sales)
  - Increasing distribution (regulatory, sales, quality, logistics)
  - Pivoting toward new product lines (supply chain, production, quality, sales)
  - Capital expenditures, especially automation (safety, maintenance/engineering, production, quality)
- Organizational decisions
  - Bringing specialist skills into the brewery as direct hires versus outsourcing
    - Dedicated maintenance or quality personnel, payroll/benefits management, HR, graphic design, marketing
  - Organizational charts
    - Where are the friction points that need additional management?

Leaders and Managers
- Compare assets versus liabilities—safety, morale, and quality should be key considerations
  - What are you doing well? Where are your pain points?
    - Are these anecdotal or backed up by objective measurements (e.g., KPIs)?
    - Are you prepared to execute on new plans/targets? If not, what needs to change?
- What is causing staff turnover?
  - Better opportunities or existing frustrations?
- What tools do you have at your disposal to make improvements?
  - Personnel, skillsets, equipment
- What do you need to track in order to be successful for the next phase?
- What is your plan for preparing your teams?

breadth and depth within its executive team. This model requires more effort than selecting a specific "heir," but it offers increased flexibility for a changing business landscape and the potential for ehigh performers to move on to other opportunities outside the current workplace.

Creating an organizational depth chart is one tool that can be used to map out potential successors for various positions within the brewery. Outside hires are always possible, perhaps even likely. This requires an in-depth understanding of the needs for future growth mapped against current capabilities, which is a callback to the initial steps outlined in chapter 1. Key factors to consider when evaluating these future leaders are the following (Berkley and Kaplan 2020, 265):

- Behavioral flexibility
- Interpersonal sensitivity
- Organizational sensitivity
- Judgment
- Perseverance
- Stress tolerance

The portfolio of skills you will need in the future depends on what challenges you anticipate facing.

PUTTING IT ALL TOGETHER
Workplace cultures need to be integrated throughout all parts of the organization. Breweries aren't defined by their stainless steel: they are the collective effort of everyone who contributes to the company's operations. This extends far beyond the brew deck. Public-facing roles like sales and hospitality staff represent the brand, while accounting, warehouse, and maintenance employees ensure that background operations go smoothly. The responsibility for generating a healthy, robust workplace culture belongs to everyone.

Leadership and management have to play an active role in order to achieve this. Clearly defined expectations are critical, and actions have to be aligned with stated priorities. Not addressing toxic or disruptive behavior sends a clear signal that the brewery's actual values don't match what is written in the handbook.

The Road to Implementation
The first six chapters present the core components needed to build and maintain an effective team. For breweries in progress, there's your roadmap. For more established breweries, there is a different challenge: where do you begin with implementing these components? To start, be honest about your needs and capabilities. Determining where your pinch points are is the most important item to start with. Are you having trouble attracting talented people or is the difficulty that you can't retain them? Are your teams self-sufficient or do they need constant supervision and support? Each of those questions point to a separate issue, so having a solid grasp on the situation is vital. It is the rare operation that has only one challenge at a time: don't get distracted from your priorities. Effective change involves fixing the problems that are causing the most disruption.

Developing and maintaining an employee handbook helps to codify information, but paperwork isn't culture. The running theme of this book has been that an organizational culture is a lived experience. Establishing and maintaining trust is essential to an effective culture. Leaders, including the owners, need to be actively engaged with their teams. Now, owners don't need to pull bartending or brewing shifts in order to be actively engaged, but they do need to cultivate an environment where the staff is confident that issues raised and communicated to management will be heard and that problems will be addressed quickly and consistently.

This kind of culture takes time to fully develop, but focusing on immediate needs will deliver tangible benefits to employees. Equally important is communicating your intentions and expectations. It's hard for employees to rally behind a plan they don't understand, much less see themselves as active participants in the process. Once you have established a clear direction and set of priorities, you need to provide the necessary resources. This may drive the sequence of events: some changes are more resource intensive than others. Again, communication is the key. Your most important project may not be accomplished quickly, but being up front about timelines makes a huge difference. In the meantime, other projects can be tackled. Progress leads to momentum, and momentum leads to continued engagement.

Leverage the Full Range of Talents Available
Building a team starts with identifying the skills and attributes your brewery needs. But you should also search for talents that hold potential beyond your

current needs. That search benefits from casting as wide a net as possible. Recruiting for potential is about skills, not familiarity.

The next challenge involves developing and retaining the people whose skills will help the brewery over the long term. This starts not with professional development, but with respecting the dignity of fellow employees, followed by consistently expecting staff to adhere to the values the brewery has identified. No matter how skilled an employee, they are a liability if they can't interact with colleagues professionally or if they represent a safety hazard to themselves or their coworkers. With cultural values as your baseline, you can move forward with investing in employees' professional development.

Resilience

Breweries occupy a special place within local communities and broader society, punching well above their economic impact. Whether a brewery sells 500 or 500,000 barrels a year, people declare an affiliation to their favorites through wearing brewery merch or buying glassware. Meanwhile, local taprooms can function as community spaces. As mentioned at the very beginning of this book, while brewery aesthetics play a role in this, the real essence of that consumer experience comes from the beer itself and the customer service. Both of these aspects come into existence through daily human activity, and that puts them in the realm of organizational culture.

Employees are the most important asset in any brewery, and while the impact may not be immediate, investing in them pays significant dividends. The culture you create and maintain governs how employees engage with their work and their colleagues. Creating a collective sense of purpose allows a brewery to be adaptable, robust, and scalable. Teams will thrive even when individuals falter. If you continually work at nurturing your brewery's culture, you will come to realize that the most important milestone for any new employee is the day they stop referring to the brewery staff as "you" and start saying "we."

APPENDIX A
ANNOTATED EXAMPLES OF JOB DESCRIPTIONS AND POSTINGS

In order to recruit necessary skills and experience into the brewery to improve your existing teams, you need to perform some preparatory work in advance:

- Understand what you're looking for in terms of filling skills gaps within the team.
- Write out the functions you need a new hire to perform.
- Organize that information so it is clear and specific: this is important for accountability.

- Communicate the target skills and experience in a way that allows qualified applicants to see themselves in the position. It's important to write this in a way that doesn't exclude people.
  - There are tools freely available that can give pointers as to whether your language is unconsciously biased (e.g., https://gender-decoder.katmatfield.com) but it is important to remember they are not meant to be prescriptive.

EXAMPLE #1: MAINTENANCE TECHNICIAN DESCRIPTION
Courtesy of SanTan Brewing Company

Maintenance Technician – SanTan Brewing Company, Chandler, AZ

The Maintenance Technician will report to the Engineering Manager and join a team of 100+ production and restaurant staff. The maintenance team typically operates between 6:00 a.m. and 6:00 p.m., on a staggered basis, but will occasionally be expected to work outside of these hours when certain projects deem it necessary. Maintenance personnel also move between our main production plant and brewpub restaurant, performing maintenance tasks at each facility.

An overview in the job description helps to place the position in the wider organization.

Essential Tasks and Responsibilities

Write out the necessary functions that you need the new position to perform. This will guide the applicant review process and interviews.

- Communicate and treat fellow coworkers and other members of the SanTan team with respect.
- Adhere to a "safety always" mindset and comply with safety policies and programs.
- Approach every task with quality in mind, paying attention to detail and accuracy.
- Perform scheduled and unscheduled maintenance and repairs on commercial kitchen/restaurant equipment, HVAC equipment, beverage packaging equipment, and brewing equipment.
- Perform building maintenance, including plumbing, electrical, and other basic construction repairs.
- Inspect, operate, and test machinery and equipment; diagnose machine malfunctions.
- Record all work performed and cost of maintenance or repair work in company computerized maintenance management system (CMMS) system, for which training will be provided.
- Repair and replace defective equipment parts, using hand tools and power tools.
- Travel between company locations to perform maintenance and repairs as needed.
- Travel to hardware stores and supply houses to procure parts and tools necessary to make repairs.
- Recommend measures to improve production methods, equipment performance, and product quality.
- Coordinate with outside vendors as needed regarding repairs or projects that are outsourced or otherwise out of the scope of the assigned duties.
- Operate heavy equipment and company vehicles as needed, including forklifts and large trucks and trailers.
- Machinery operation and repair may require the use of safety equipment, including, but not limited to: eye safety glasses, hearing protection, work boots, hard hats, and energy lockout/tagout (LOTO) equipment.
- The employee may be required to understand the work of other departments and assist them when needed.

All production employees are expected to be able to:
- Maintain a strong focus on quality, safety and efficiency, constantly evaluating work practices in the spirit of "always improving"
- Communicate effectively and openly with team members
- Work in factory and kitchen/restaurant environments that may be loud, hot, cold, humid, or have wet/slippery floors
- Multitask and follow standard operating procedures
- Manipulate valves, clamps, and hoses as necessary
- Operate hand and power tools safely and efficiently
- Bend, crawl, twist, turn, lift, kneel, and climb ladders and stairs
- Stand for prolonged periods
- Work indoors, outdoors, and on rooftops when necessary
- Work safely with chemicals of varying composition, including wearing personal protection equipment such as gloves and goggles
- Safely work at height on ladders and elevated platforms
- Safely work in and around confined spaces
- Operate a pallet jack and complete forklift certification
- Regularly lift/carry heavy objects up to 55 lb. repeatedly and safely above waist level
- Occasionally move heavy objects up to 165 lb.

Lay out the skill sets and experiences that a qualified applicant would have in order to successfully perform the required tasks.

Qualifications
- Experience with troubleshooting in complex and time-sensitive environments
- Mechanical aptitude and a moderate understanding of mechanical systems
- 2+ years' experience in manufacturing maintenance, including electrical, plumbing, HVAC, pneumatics, welding, and cutting. Basic knowledge of programmable logic controller (PLC) and relay logic preferred
- Education: HS diploma; trades knowledge and experience
- Flexible work schedule: available to work all shifts, additional hours and weekends as necessary

Providing a pay scale is normally part of the posting, but including it in the job description from the start helps to make sure everyone is on the same page when budgeting for the position.

Benefits and Compensation
The Maintenance Technician position is a full-time role with a pay scale between $XX,XXX and $XX,XXX (depending on experience) and full-time benefits package.

EXAMPLE #2: LEADERSHIP/MANAGEMENT POSTING

Courtesy of Fair State Brewing Company

Description of the brewery to provide geographic and background context for the posting

Fair State Brewing Cooperative is seeking a New Product Development Manager to join our staffs across two sites in Northeast Minneapolis and in St. Paul, MN.

Fair State is one of a limited number of cooperatively owned breweries in the US. We began operations at our Northeast Minneapolis brewery and taproom in August 2014, and added a production brewery in St. Paul in 2017.

Quick overview of the position and reporting structure

The New Product Development Manager plays a key role at Fair State, being responsible for the ideation and formulation of new beer, non-alcoholic (NA), and CBD/THC products, and acting as the point of contact for co-packing and contract partners. The New Product Development Manager will have an active role at both of our facilities: directly supervising the Innovation Brewer and assuming some brewery management tasks at our taproom brewery in NE Minneapolis; and working with the rest of the production management team at our St. Paul brewery to bring our brand calendar to life.

This position reports to the Head Brewer, but the role will involve working closely with all of production management, as well as department heads in Marketing/Design and Retail.

Core responsibilities. Note the clarity and specificity: this is important for highly tailored leadership positions.

Responsibilities

- Develop annual brand calendar for year-round products, variety packs, and monthly limited releases, including recipes and accurate costing information
- Manage all New Product Development communication between the entire management team and ensure new products stay on track for release dates
- Work with Marketing/Design and Sales to provide context and support for products in-market
- Be responsible for developing new NA products, such as NA beers, hop waters, and CBD/THC products
- Supervise the Innovation Brewer at the NE Minneapolis taproom and work with production management to ensure smooth operation of the NE Minneapolis brewery
- Work closely with the Innovation Brewer and the Retail Director to populate the brewery-only release calendar
- Act as point of contact for contract and co-packing partners, ensuring the right questions are going to the right people at the right time
- Effectively communicate all things New Product Development internally to staff, and externally via interviews, podcasts, etc., as needed
- Maintain the New Product Development budget

Clearly lays out what they are looking for in an ideal candidate; all are relevant to the actual position

Desired Skills and Experience

- 2+ years in the brewing industry—strong preference for previous production management experience
- Proven track record of recipe development and successful product launches
- Knowledge and understanding of NA beer, CBD/THC, and other NA product categories
- Creative, open-minded, curious, and able to master new processes quickly
- Strong verbal and written communication skills
- Organized, detail-oriented, and able to juggle multiple things
- Experience with Microsoft Office products; experience with OrchestratedBEER preferred

Requirements

- At least 21 years of age at time of application
- Able to stand for prolonged periods
- Able to stoop, crawl, twist, turn, lift, kneel, and climb ladders and stairs
- Able to manipulate valves and clamps
- Able to regularly lift/carry heavy objects up to 55 lb. repeatedly and safely above waist level
- Able to occasionally move very heavy objects up to 165 lb.
- Able to work in a factory environment that may be loud, hot, humid, cold, or slick
- Able to work in a fast-paced environment with high-pressure deadlines and time constraints
- Able to comply with safe chemical handling procedures, including personal protection equipment such as gloves and goggles
- Able to safely work on ladders and elevated platforms and in confined spaces
- Able to safely operate vehicles and material handling equipment (e.g., vans, trucks, hand trucks, scissor lifts, forklifts, pallet jacks)
  - Possess a valid driver's license and ability to pass insurance driving record review for operating company-owned vehicles on public roads

Compensation and Benefits

This is a full-time, salaried position compensated at $XX,XXX–$XX,XXX annually. As a full-time employee, this role is also eligible for:

- 8 paid holidays (New Year's Day, Memorial Day, Juneteenth, Independence Day, Labor Day, Thanksgiving Day, the day after Thanksgiving, and Christmas Day)
- Paid time off (PTO), which can be used for any purpose and is accrued at a rate of 0.0769 hours of PTO per hour worked (up to 4 weeks per year)
- Paid parental leave (160 hours of paid parental leave in the 12 months following, or the 9 months prior to, the birth, adoption, or foster placement of a child in your home)
- Health insurance for employee, spouse/domestic partner, and dependents, with a portion of premiums paid by Fair State
- Dental and vision insurance, with 50% of employee and dependent premiums paid by Fair State
- Short-Term and Long-Term Disability, Accidental Death & Dismemberment, and life insurance coverage, with 100% of premiums paid by Fair State
- Flexible savings account for medical and dependent care
- Simple IRA with employer-matching up to 3% (eligible in 2023)
- Employee Assistance Program
- Discounted membership in our cooperative (after 6 months)
- Credit for Fair State clothing merchandise at hire
- Annual safety clothing and equipment stipend
- Employee beer stipend
- Fair State merchandise and beer discounts

Explain the process and timing for applicants, as well as proactively encouraging a wide range of applicants

Application Process

To apply, email a resume and cover letter to <contact email>. Applications will be accepted until <opening date> and interviews will be conducted on a rolling basis. We're looking for someone to start by <starting date>.

Studies have shown that women and people of color are less likely to apply for jobs unless they believe they meet every one of the qualifications as described in a job description. We are most interested in finding the best candidate for the job. We would encourage you to apply, even if you don't believe you meet every one of our qualifications described. If you are unsure whether you meet the qualifications of this position, or how this would be determined, please feel free to contact <contact email> to discuss your application.

Equal Employment Opportunity

Fair State Brewing Cooperative strongly supports equal employment opportunity for all applicants regardless of race, color, religion, sex, gender identity, pregnancy, national origin, ancestry, citizenship, age, marital status, physical disability, mental disability, medical condition, sexual orientation, genetic information, or any other characteristic protected by state or federal law.

APPENDIX B
EXAMPLE NEEDS ASSESSMENT AND JOB DESCRIPTION PAIRING

The following template describes the writing process of a job description for an entry-level brewery production position.

NEEDS ASSESSMENT

Context and Background
- Taproom-model brewery with limited keg and crowler distribution
- 10 bbl. brewhouse
- Annual volume: 850 bbl./year (current)
- Goals:
  - 1,000 bbl./year (next year)
  - 1,600 bbl./year within 4 years
  - Existing structure would max out at 2,200 bbl./year

Priorities: What do we need to accomplish the goals?
- Increase weekly production
  - Brewed batches, cellar management
  - Packaged beer
- Increase capacity for active troubleshooting
  - Reduce round-the-clock demand on the Head Brewer's availability
  - Reduce service calls from contractors for routine maintenance
- Develop expertise for future growth and flexibility

Needs: What are we hiring for?
Immediate needs
- Support existing production group
  - Routine brew production and packaging work
  - Reduce potential for burnout
- Troubleshooting and problem-solving skills
  - Manual brewery, so mechanical skills would be ideal, but finding a candidate comfortable with do-it-yourself (DIY) projects is the emphasis

Long-term needs
- Growth plan won't require particularly high-speed or specialized equipment, but general lab skills will improve quality through reduced waste
- Leadership potential is a plus: a lot can change in 3–4 years

Ideal candidate: What are we looking for?
- Experience in fast-paced and team-oriented work environments
- Experience with troubleshooting and problem-solving in time-sensitive environments
- Mechanical aptitude and a basic understanding of mechanical systems
- Flexible work schedule—able to do early mornings or weekend shifts as necessary
- Preferred experience, but not necessary:
  - 1+ years in the brewing industry or a related field
  - Fermentation/brewing degree or certificate from an accredited program

JOB DESCRIPTION

Assistant Brewer

The Assistant Brewer will report to the Head Brewer. This is an entry-level position, and training will be provided where necessary. The brewing team typically operates during weekdays between 5:00 a.m. and 2:00 p.m., although occasional weekend shifts may be needed depending on workflow. The Assistant Brewer will move between brewhouse, cellar, and packaging duties, providing support to the rest of the brewery team.

Core Responsibilities

- Communicate and treat fellow coworkers and brewery partners and guests with respect
- Adhere to a "safety always" mindset and comply with safety policies and programs
- Approach every task with quality in mind, paying attention to detail and accuracy
- Maintain a clean and organized workspace in accordance with food safety regulations
- Clean and sanitize all vessels (brewhouse vessels, fermentors, bright beer tanks, and packaging equipment)
- Operate a 10 bbl. brewhouse (milling, wort production)
- Perform fermentation tank management (sanitary technique, gravity checks, trub dumps, dry hopping, etc.)
- Perform yeast management tasks (harvesting, pitching, and counts/viabilities)
- Perform beer filtration and finishing tasks with attention to sanitary technique, clarity, yield, and carbonation accuracy
- Package finished beer into kegs and cans with particular emphasis on safety and quality
- Participate in sensory evaluation panels
- Assist with preventative maintenance tasks
- Ensure that paperwork and associated reporting is done accurately and on time
- Maintain an inventory of raw materials and brewery supplies, including receiving materials
- Troubleshooting, technical maintenance, and quality assurance
- Understand and be able to assist other departments when needed

All employees are expected to be able to:

- Maintain a strong focus on quality, safety, and efficiency, constantly evaluating work practices in the spirit of "always improving"
- Communicate effectively and openly with team members
- Work in a factory environment that may be loud, hot, humid, or have wet/slippery floors
- Multitask and follow standard operating procedures
- Manipulate valves and clamps
- Use measuring and diagnostic equipment (e.g., pH meters, microscopes, dissolved oxygen meters, etc.)
- Bend, crawl, twist, turn, lift, kneel, and climb ladders and stairs
- Stand for prolonged periods
- Work safely with chemicals of varying composition, including wearing personal protection equipment such as gloves and goggles
- Safely work at height on ladders and elevated platforms
- Safely work in and around confined spaces
- Operate a pallet jack and complete forklift certification
- Regularly lift/carry heavy objects up to 55 lb. repeatedly and safely above waist level
- Occasionally move heavy objects up to 165 lb.

Desired Qualifications and Experience
- Experience in fast-paced and team-oriented work environments
- Experience with troubleshooting and problem-solving in time-sensitive environments
- Mechanical aptitude and a basic understanding of mechanical systems
- Flexible work schedule—able to work early mornings or weekend shifts as necessary

Preferred Experience
- 1+ years in the brewing industry or a related field
- Fermentation/brewing degree or certificate from an accredited program

Benefits and Compensation
The Assistant Brewer position is a full-time, non-exempt role with a pay rate between $17/hour and $21/hour (depending on experience) with full-time benefits.

APPENDIX C
SAMPLE INTERVIEW QUESTIONS

The following questions are designed to be open-ended and applicable to almost any role within a brewery. These questions are also more accessible to candidates from a broad range of previous work and educational backgrounds by not using jargon or requiring specialized knowledge.

More detailed questions can be included to learn more about experience with and approaches to safety, quality, customer service, and specific job-related knowledge, but this set of questions will shed light on how well a candidate matches your brewery's values and has the aptitude and attitude you've identified as important.

SAMPLE QUESTIONS

Please take me through your recent work history and provide a brief overview of what you learned from each position. Of those most applicable for this role, how did they lead you to where you are today?

- Purpose: Résumés can only say so much. Get a sense of the applicant's experience and let them describe their career arc in their own words. Follow up on career transitions and assess their adaptability. Do they share the brewery's core values or are there red flags?

Walk us through a typical day or week at your current job (or the position that best matches this job posting).

- Purpose: Are they engaged with their work? This isn't about being passionate about a job they're interested in leaving, but rather what they prioritize in their work in general.

What are the most important tasks at your job? What makes them so important?

- Purpose: Useful follow up to the previous question to gain more clarity on the applicant's work values and priorities.

What is it about this role that motivated you to apply?

- Purpose: Determine what it is about this role they are passionate about and what interests them about the brewery. Look for mismatches between the candidate's expectations and the realities of the role.

Describe to me the type of work environment you thrive in, and why?

- Purpose: What is the applicant looking for in a job? Ask follow-up questions to get a sense of whether they understand the work environment and can adapt to your brewery's core values and priorities.

Tell me about a time when you had to make a time-sensitive decision based on limited information. What was the situation and how did you influence the process?

- Purpose: Get to know the applicant's communication style and how they deal with their peers.

Tell us about a time you were part of a successful team. What was your role on that team?

- Purpose: How does the applicant approach team dynamics? Are they comfortable in team-based environments?

Based on what this role entails, tell me how you would add value right away?

- Purpose: Confirm whether the applicant understands the role and can identify key attributes needed to be successful.

What other areas of education or training have you had that would be relevant to this position?

- Purpose: This is an opportunity to draw out additional problem-solving and other work-relevant skills and talents.

What questions do you have for me, either about the role or the company overall?

- Purpose: Is the applicant an active participant in the interview or just going through the motions? Are they making an informed decision on their end?

INTERVIEW QUESTIONNAIRE

Position: [POSITION_NAME]	
Interview: [Phone] [In-person]	
Name	**Date/Time**

Rating	Rating definition & methodology
4	Highly qualified / solid aptitude fit
3	Qualified / likely aptitude fit
2	Some transferable experience / can be trained
1	Not qualified / not a good fit

- **Please take me through your work history and provide a brief overview of what you learned from each position and how they led you to where you are today.**

- **Walk us through a typical day or week at your current job (or the position that best matches this job posting).**

- What are the most important tasks at your job? What makes them so important?

- What is it about this role that motivated you to apply?

- Describe to me the type of work environment you thrive in, and why?

- Tell me about a time when you had to make a time-sensitive decision based on limited information. What was the situation and how did you influence the process?

- Based on what this role entails, tell me how you would add value right away?

- What questions do you have for me, either about the role or the company overall?

APPENDIX D
SAMPLE PRODUCTION TRAINING CHECKLIST FOR BREWING

This checklist is designed to lay out the expected skills progression for a new hire over an eight-week training cycle. The first week is dedicated to orientation, with the second week focused on general production skills and awareness. The following weeks are split into sections for hot-side (brew deck) and cold-side (cellar) operations.

In practice, a new hire will be involved in a wider range of tasks than those listed for a specific week.

The goal of this progression is to clearly lay out what you need them to focus on and when. The employee will be involved with boiling and knocking out wort in Weeks 3–4, but they won't be assessed on proficiency until Week 6. If they learn faster, wonderful, but don't put them in a position to be overwhelmed.

Likewise, hot-side and cold-side operations may be combined to suit your production realities. Just build out a progression that lays out the objectives for each week, mixing and matching as needed.

WEEK 1: ORIENTATION

Administrative Components
- Housekeeping tour: Identify building locations
  - ❏ Entry/exits
  - ❏ Restrooms
  - ❏ Breakroom/personal storage area
  - ❏ Offices
- Human resources: Deliver and/or demonstrate core HR functions
  - ❏ Hiring paperwork (I-9, emergency contacts, etc.)
  - ❏ Handbook
  - ❏ Timecard/punch system
  - ❏ Key fobs/door keys
  - ❏ IT setup (email and other system logins)
  - ❏ Key personnel contact information
  - ❏ Sick/PTO call-in procedure
- Manager goals and expectations:
  - ❏ Review training process and manager priorities and expectations
  - ❏ Explain what success looks like within the department
- Key contacts:
  - ❏ Introduce employees to department managers and other key personnel
- Taproom rules: Go over the rights and responsibilities of employees in the brewery taproom; we recommend covering:
  - ❏ Shift beers
  - ❏ Ordering beers
  - ❏ "Friends and family" rules
  - ❏ Coffee service etiquette
  - ❏ Use of space as a breakroom and/or office/meeting room, etc.)
- Manager review:
  - ❏ End-of-week review
  - ❏ Discuss the upcoming training schedule

Culture
- Brewery identity: Discuss the history and mission; what makes you "you"?
  - ❏ History
  - ❏ Mission/value statement
  - ❏ Goals
  - ❏ Place the brewery in the local/regional/national context
- Brewery tour: Walk employees through a VIP-style brewery tour
  - ❏ Basic brewing process overview
  - ❏ Taproom and location highlights
  - ❏ Q&A
- Brand portfolio overview: Broad-strokes discussion of the flavor profile and concepts of the beer portfolio
  - ❏ Core brands
  - ❏ Seasonal/specialty

Production Tasks

- Job-shadowing: Watch operations to gain a sense of the overall process and build familiarity with the space before active training begins. Emphasis should be on safety and general workflow
  - ❏ Beer production
    - ▪ Hot side
    - ▪ Cold side
  - ❏ Beer packaging
- SOP class and system overview:
  - ❏ Workspace: Review parts and raw material storage areas
  - ❏ Review SOP format
  - ❏ Walk through basic piping and equipment
    - ▪ Process and instrument diagram (P&ID)
  - ❏ Introduce equipment/machine controls

Safety and Awareness

- Safety overview: Review core safety material required for the "Affected Employee" category
  - ❏ Safety program overview and Personal Protective Equipment (PPE)
  - ❏ Safety hierarchy of controls
  - ❏ Hazard communication/right-to-know
  - ❏ Basic emergency response

NOTE: Don't forget to maintain training logs on safety material

- Food safety overview: Review core requirements of the Good Manufacturing Practices (GMP) program
  - ❏ GMP program overview

NOTE: Don't forget to maintain training logs on safety material

- Building walkthrough
  - ❏ Identify chemical storage areas and other brewery hazards
  - ❏ Locations of emergency eyewashes, fire extinguishers, and fire exits
- Authorized staff training
  - ❏ Review core safety concepts via Brewers Association video series and Master Brewers Toolbox Talks (assign specific topics based on site-specific material listed in Week 2)
- Industrial lift training: Forklifts, scissors lifts, powered pallet jacks
  - ❏ Classroom phase
  - ❏ Practical phase

Trainer Signature: _____ Date_____

Employee Signature: _____ Date_____

WEEK 2: CORE COMPETENCIES—GENERAL OPERATIONS

- Morning start-up processes
  - ❏ Show, practice, demonstrate
- Process and instrumentation diagram (P&ID):
  - ❏ Take the time to learn the process flow in the brewhouse and fermentation cellar
  - ❏ Demonstrate knowledge by requiring trainees to trace each flow

NOTE: Expectation is not showing that employee knows how to correctly set up the lines yet. The aim is for them to understand and recognize the basic process flows:

- Cold water
- Hot water
- Wort knock-out
- Vessel clean-in-place (CIP)/sanitation loops
- Carbon dioxide (CO_2) lines
- Filtration hose train
- Packaging hose train
- Water and CO_2 drops in the brewery

- Theory section—Cleaning and sanitation: train staff on the fundamentals; don't assume that people already know the material
  - ❏ Cleaning
    - Chemical action
    - Mechanical action
    - Time
    - Temperature
    - Safety: Incompatible materials
  - ❏ Sanitation
    - Chemical action
    - Mechanical action
    - Effective contact time (remember, it isn't instant)
    - Rinse versus no-rinse procedures and concentrations
    - Safety: Incompatible materials
- Good Manufacturing Practices (GMPs)
  - ❏ Handwash sinks
  - ❏ Rules for personal consumption in the production area
- Safety: Train for on site-specific requirements
  - ❏ Hazard communication
  - ❏ Chemical handling
  - ❏ Lockout/tagout (LOTO)
  - ❏ Confined space entry programs (CSEP)
  - ❏ Hot liquids and surfaces
  - ❏ Personal protective equipment (PPE)
  - ❏ Pressurized vessels
  - ❏ CO_2 management
  - ❏ Ergonomics
  - ❏ Forklifts
  - ❏ Ladders and fall prevention

- Brewery software and record-keeping
  - ❑ Log in
  - ❑ Navigate data entry forms
  - ❑ Correctly enter data
- Raw material storage locations
  - ❑ Malt
  - ❑ Hops
  - ❑ CIP/sanitation chemicals
  - ❑ Housekeeping chemicals
  - ❑ Filtration process aids

Trainer Signature: _____ Date_____

Employee Signature: _____ Date_____

WEEKS 3–4: CORE COMPETENCIES—COLD SIDE

- Work area housekeeping: Master the basic organization and regular cleaning requirements in the brewery; for example:
  - ❑ Daily—cleaning parts storage and chemical storage areas, hose organization, spill clean-up, clean buckets, etc.
  - ❑ Weekly—scrub drain and grates, scrub tank legs and feet, prepare packaging area for following week
- Theory section—Fermentation process: train staff on the fundamentals; don't assume that people already know the material
  - ❑ Primary fermentation
  - ❑ Warm maturation phase
  - ❑ Cold maturation phase
  - ❑ Fermentation measurements
    - ▪ What the measurements mean and why we check
- Process logs: Learn the terminology and purpose of each log. Understand how the logs are formatted, how to enter data, and how to recognize problems
  - ❑ Brew sheets
  - ❑ Fermentation log
  - ❑ Packaging log
  - ❑ Sanitation book
- Daily measurements: Learn the steps for each daily fermentation measurement. Focus on proper technique, recognizing anomalies, and data entry
  - ❑ Proper sampling technique with an emphasis on sanitation and cleanup
  - ❑ Gravities
  - ❑ pH
  - ❑ Temperature checks
- Fermentation profiles for the portfolio: Learn the target values along with control and action limits for key parameters
  - ❑ OG/FG
  - ❑ Temperatures
  - ❑ Fermentation profiles/curves

- Chemical measurement and titrations
  - ❏ Learn the target concentration for CIP and sanitizer compounds
    - ▪ Understand where to look up this information when in doubt
  - ❏ Learn how to safely pump or pour chemicals from bulk and secondary containers
    - ▪ Container rinsing
    - ▪ PPE requirements
    - ▪ Minor spill cleanup
  - ❏ Protocol for mixing chemicals
    - ▪ Always add concentrate to water, never the reverse
  - ❏ Learn the steps for titrating working strength solutions

NOTE: Corrective actions/measures will be covered in following weeks—focus on the steps for now

- Tank setup and teardown: Learn and master the sequences for these tasks
  - ❏ Fermentors
  - ❏ Bright beer tanks (BBTs)
  - ❏ Balance lines (or equivalent)
- Hose setup
  - ❏ Learn and master the sequences for these tasks
- CIP/clean-out-of-place (COP) and sanitation: Learn and master the sequences for these tasks
  - ❏ Understand the purpose and objective
    - ▪ Define terms
    - ▪ Distinction between "cleaning" and "sanitizing"
  - ❏ **Safety note:** Pay particular attention to chemical, heat, and pressure hazards
  - ❏ **Quality note:** Impress upon the group how important proper technique and contact time are
  - ❏ Parts
  - ❏ Hose loops
  - ❏ Vessels and equipment
- Adenosine triphosphate (ATP) testing/monitoring
  - ❏ Understand what this instrument measures and what information it gives you
  - ❏ Site selection for testing
  - ❏ Testing technique
  - ❏ Data entry
- Tank bunging
  - ❏ Understand the purpose and objective of bunging a tank
  - ❏ Required conditions for bunging
  - ❏ Learn proper steps

Trainer Signature: _____ Date_____

Employee Signature: _____ Date_____

WEEK 5–6: CORE COMPETENCIES—COLD SIDE

- Work area housekeeping: Master the expanded organization and regular cleaning requirements in the brewery; for example:
  - ❏ Monthly—organizing and cleaning storage areas, checking safety showers and fire extinguishers, foaming vessel exteriors and floors
- Corrective actions: Learn the proper adjustments for measurements that are out of spec
  - ❏ CIP and sanitizer titrations
  - ❏ ATP results
  - ❏ Leaks from hoses, pumps, or vessels
  - ❏ Fermentation and BBT temperatures
  - ❏ Carbonation
  - ❏ Dissolved O_2 (DO)
- Sensory: Learn to recognize the normal range of flavors associated with fermenting and finished beer
  - ❏ In-process beer:
    - ▪ What is normal versus abnormal for actively fermenting beer (aroma, color, flavor) at each stage of the process?
  - ❏ Finished beer:
    - ▪ Learn the target primary and secondary flavor characteristics for each brand
    - ▪ Understand the accepted flavor range that is considered "true to brand"
- Dry-hopping process: Learn and master the process steps
  - ❏ **Safety**
    - ▪ Ladder set-up & security, climbing, and load-lifting technique
    - ▪ Carbonation/CO_2 release
  - ❏ **Quality**
    - ▪ Sanitation of parts and work area
- Vicinal diketone (VDK) testing—diacetyl
  - ❏ Understand what this is measuring
  - ❏ Sample technique
  - ❏ Sample preparation and testing
  - ❏ Sensory evaluation
  - ❏ Data entry
- Yeast management
  - ❏ Harvest strategy
  - ❏ Harvest process
  - ❏ Fassing/yeast dumps
- CO_2 purging
  - ❏ Understand the purpose and objective: removing oxygen from a vessel by creating a dense layer of CO_2 to prevent DO pickup
  - ❏ Preparation of the vessel and purging rig
    - ▪ Emphasis on sanitation
  - ❏ Process steps
    - ▪ Flowrate and duration
  - ❏ Purge validation
- Carbonation
  - ❏ Understand the purpose and objective: safely carbonating beer to the target level under sanitary conditions
  - ❏ Preparation of the vessel and purging rig
    - ▪ Emphasis on sanitation

- ❏ Process steps
  - ▪ Flowrate and duration
- ❏ Purge validation
- • Filtration
- ❏ Understand the purpose and objective: safely filtering beer to the target haze level under sanitary conditions and with minimal DO pickup
- ❏ **Safety**
  - ▪ Manage pressurized vessels
  - ▪ Handling filtration aids, e.g., diatomaceous earth, polyvinylpolypyrrolidone (PVPP)
- ❏ **Quality**
  - ▪ Sanitation
  - ▪ Preventing DO pickup
- ❏ Setup
- ❏ Process
- ❏ Teardown and cleanup

Trainer Signature: _____ Date_____

Employee Signature: _____ Date_____

WEEKS 7–8: COMPETENCY AND TRAINING REVIEW—COLD SIDE

Goals for these weeks are to:
- • identify and address any training areas that may have been missed or not thoroughly understood;
- • provide time for operators to progress from basic understanding to full competency through repetition and practice;
- • make the determination whether operators are prepared to function without active supervision.

Trainer Signature: _____ Date_____

Employee Signature: _____ Date_____

WEEKS 3–4: CORE COMPETENCIES—HOT SIDE

- Work area housekeeping
  - ❏ Daily—spill cleanup, hose organization, and sweeping mill room and storage areas
  - ❏ Weekly—scrub drains and grates, detail mill room, clean grain and hop storage, etc.
- Theory section—Brewhouse processes I: train staff on the fundamentals; don't assume that people already know the material
  - ❏ Mash objectives
    - ▪ Enzyme activity: importance of temperature targets
  - ❏ Lautering objectives
    - ▪ Balancing speed versus efficiency
- Process logs: Learn the terminology and purpose of each log. Understand how the logs are formatted, how to enter data, and how to recognize problems
  - ❏ Brew sheets
  - ❏ Fermentation log
  - ❏ Sanitation book
- Process measurements: Learn the steps for brewhouse measurements. Focus on proper technique, recognizing anomalies, and data entry
  - ❏ Proper sampling technique with an emphasis on safety and cleanup
  - ❏ Gravities
  - ❏ pH
  - ❏ Temperature checks
- Brewhouse profiles for the portfolio: Learn the target values along with control and action limits for key parameters
- Chemical measurement and titrations
  - ❏ Learn the target concentration for CIP compounds
    - ▪ Understand where to look up this information when in doubt.
  - ❏ Learn how to safely pump or pour chemicals from bulk and secondary containers
    - ▪ Container rinsing
    - ▪ PPE requirements
    - ▪ Minor spill cleanup
  - ❏ Protocol for mixing chemicals
    - ▪ Always add concentrate to water, never the reverse
  - ❏ Learn the steps for titrating working strength solutions

NOTE: Corrective actions/measures will be covered in following weeks—focus on the steps for now

- Sensory: Establish what is normal—off-flavor diagnosis will come later
  - ❏ Water
  - ❏ Malt
  - ❏ Hops
- Raw material management
  - ❏ Measurement
  - ❏ Storage
  - ❏ Batch documentation
- Milling
- Mashing
- Lautering

Trainer Signature: _____ Date_____

Employee Signature: _____ Date_____

WEEKS 5–6: CORE COMPETENCIES—HOT SIDE

- Theory section—Brewhouse processes II: train staff on the fundamentals; don't assume that people already know the material
  - ❏ Boiling objectives
    - ▪ Sterilize wort, concentrate sugars, convert hop acids, drive off flavor-negative volatiles
  - ❏ Hop mechanics and trade-offs
    - ▪ Bitterness: converting hop alpha acids to wort bitterness
    - ▪ Aromas: essential oils versus time and temperature
  - ❏ Whirlpool and knock-out objectives
    - ▪ Remove trub, prevent dimethyl sulfide (DMS) pickup, cool wort, oxygen addition, sanitary procedures
- Boil kettle and whirlpool procedures
- Knock-out setup and teardown
- Heat exchanger
  - ❏ Process
  - ❏ Hot liquor tank (HLT) and cold liquor tank (CLT) management
  - ❏ Backflushing
- O_2/aeration
- Yeast management
  - ❏ Viability
  - ❏ Pitch rate calculations
  - ❏ Pitching
- CIP and sanitation
- Corrective actions/measures

Trainer Signature: _____ Date_____

Employee Signature: _____ Date_____

WEEKS 7–8: COMPETENCY AND TRAINING REVIEW—HOT SIDE

Goals for these weeks are to:
- identify and address any training areas that may have been missed or not thoroughly understood;
- provide time for operators to progress from basic understanding to full competency through repetition and practice;
- make the determination whether operators are prepared to function without active supervision.

Trainer Signature: _____ Date_____

Employee Signature: _____ Date_____

APPENDIX E
SAMPLE TRAINING CHECKLIST FOR TAPROOM STAFF

Courtesy of Kat Schermerhorn, General Manager, Jackalope Brewing

This checklist is designed to lay out the expected skills progression for a new bartender/server over a training cycle comprising five shifts.

3-4 shifts before full tips
- 1 opening shift
- 1 closing shift
- 1 weekend shift (if possible)
- 1 open-to-close shift (if possible)
  - 1 mid-shift is OK if it is the only option

ORIENTATION

(Approx. 2–3 hours)

- Paperwork
- Handbook materials: focus on policies, benefits, etc.
- Job description overview and expectations
  - If the brewery engages with delivery services, cover this as well
- Cover the scheduling process (app or printout) and clock-in number
- Training schedule overview; give expectations of trainee and trainer and all training materials
- Uniform and tour (include parking)
- Taproom's I.D. policy
- Alcohol Intervention Procedure certification (TIPS, ServSafe, etc.)
- Beer tasting (year-round and seasonals)
- Brewery history

TRAINING SHIFT #1

Following shift lead. Trainer will always explain the why behind the method.

Weekday: full open-to-close shift.
Weekend: full open or full close shift (no mid-shifts).

Focus
- Tour of specific workspaces
- Where things live (and why they live there)
- Basic opening/closing procedures
- Listening to lead talk about beers with guests
- Glassware and pouring beers
- Changing kegs
- Packing orders and delivery orders
- Point-of-sale (POS) system
- Importance of the bar log
- **CHECKLISTS:** Heavy focus on these

TRAINING SHIFT #2

Following shift lead. Trainer will still do most of the talking with guests.

Weekday: full open-to-close shift.
Weekend: full open or full close shift (no mid-shifts).

Focus
- Working the register/point-of-sale (POS) system: trainee will do all of the ringing up of the items, starting tabs, closing out, money, etc. while the trainer talks
- Discounts and quirks of the cash register
- Merchandise: thorough overview of it all, where things all live, backstock, rubber band sizing system, register names versus tag names, etc.
- Food preparation and prep room organization
- Side work
- Delivery orders system: who takes, when to take, and the procedure
- **CHECKLISTS:** Heavy focus on these

TRAINING SHIFT #3

Trainee takes the lead. Trainer will follow the trainee around helping and stepping in when needed.

Focus
- Guests: Trainee will do all of the talking. Trainer is listening and correcting/giving feedback in the moment and filling in the gaps for customers when needed
- Working the register/POS system: Trainee will do all of the ringing up of the items while the trainer observes.
- Opening or closing tasks: trainee takes the lead (if possible); trainer informs the trainee when it's time to start tasks (closing) or helps organize the timing of tasks (opening) for efficiency
- Food preparation and running food
- **CHECKLISTS:** trainee should be referring to these and showing trainer that they are actively using them

TRAINING SHIFT #4

Trainee takes the lead. Trainer will follow the trainee around in observation and feedback only. The trainer should not take over unless absolutely necessary.

Trainer should explain the following systems:
- Dock sales and donations procedures
- Weekly and biweekly deliveries: how we receive materials from suppliers, inventory, and store them, etc.
- Tours: how they work, how to sign up for them, etc.
- Private events: who works them and when the trainee can start working them
- Where do invoices, checks, tour certificates, etc. live?
- Phone tree: what calls go where
- Emergency contact info: trainer goes over scenarios on what to do in sticky situations

SHIFT #5

HOORAY! FULL TIPS

FOLLOW-UPS

1-month check-in: Feedback on what's going great. Clarification on things that they are struggling with.
3-month check-in: Feedback
12-month check-in: Full review

APPENDIX F
SAMPLE ONBOARDING TEMPLATE FOR BEER PACKAGING TEAM

Following is an example of a template for onboarding a new beer packaging team member. It can be customized as needed to fit your operation.

Table F.1 **Week One**

	Intro & Culture	Safety & GMPs	Team Awareness	Job-Shadowing	Job-Shadowing	
	Monday	**Tuesday**	**Wednesday**	**Thursday**	**Friday**	
7:00						7:00
7:30						7:30
8:00						8:00
8:30		Manager check-in	Manager check-in	Manager check-in		8:30
9:00	Arrival & housekeeping tour	Safety: Authorized staff training (LOTO, CSEP, and rest of BA safety videos)	Job-shadowing: Beer packaging team (emphasis on safety & overall workflow)	Industrial lift certification: Classroom & practical	Job-shadowing: Beer packaging team (emphasis on safety & overall workflow)	9:00
9:30	HR: Handbook, timecards, IT setup					9:30
10:00						10:00
10:30	Manager: Goals & expectations	Safety: Authorized staff training (site-specific phase)		SOP class & packaging systems orientation: Safety, P&ID, machine controls		10:30
11:00	Culture: Who we are and why we do what we do					11:00
11:30						11:30
12:00	Lunch	Lunch	Lunch (time may change)	Lunch (time may change)	Lunch (time may change)	12:00
12:30	Take a moment to absorb it all	Take a moment to absorb it all	FLEX/BUFFER TIME			12:30
1:00	Safety orientation: Basic programs & hazard communication	Departmental key contacts				1:00
1:30		GMP orientation: Awareness & programs			Job-shadowing: Beer packaging team (emphasis on safety & overall workflow)	1:30
2:00	Safety: Building walkthrough			Job-shadowing: Beer packaging team (emphasis on safety & overall workflow)		2:00
2:30	Brewery/facility tour	Housekeeping/ storage Tour: Where is everything kept and how is the space maintained in good working order	Job-shadowing: Beer packaging team (emphasis on safety & overall workflow)			2:30
3:00						3:00
3:30						3:30
4:00	Brand overview & sensory: Core brands	Brand overview & sensory: Seasonal/ specialty brands			Manager: Review week & next steps	4:00
4:30						4:30
5:00						5:00
5:30						5:30
6:00						6:00
6:30						6:30
7:00						7:00
7:30						7:30
8:30						8:30

Table F.2 **Week Two**

	On-the-Job-Training					
	Monday	**Tuesday**	**Wednesday**	**Thursday**	**Friday**	
7:00						7:00
7:30	Manager check-in	Manager check-in	Manager check-in	Manager check-in	Manager check-in	7:30
8:00	On-the-job training (OTJ): Emphasis on material storage locations, ergonomics, and general safety	OTJ: Emphasis on ergonomics, safety, and pallet stacking patterns	OTJ: Emphasis on safety and sanitary set-up	OTJ: Emphasis on safety, sanitation, and P&ID	OTJ: Emphasis on safety, sanitation, and P&ID	8:00
8:30						8:30
9:00						9:00
9:30						9:30
10:00						10:00
10:30						10:30
11:00	Lunch	Lunch	Lunch	Lunch	Lunch	11:00
11:30	OTJ: Emphasis on material storage locations, ergonomics, and general safety	OTJ: Emphasis on ergonomics, safety, basic CIP setup, and post-run cleanup	OTJ: Emphasis on ergonomics, safety, basic CIP setup, and post-run cleanup	OTJ: Emphasis on ergonomics, safety, basic CIP setup, and post-run cleanup	OTJ: Emphasis on safety, end-of-week cleanup	11:30
12:00						12:00
12:30						12:30
1:00						1:00
1:30						1:30
2:00						2:00
2:30						2:30
3:00						3:00
3:30						3:30
4:00					Manager check-in: Week review	4:00
4:30						4:30
5:00						5:00
5:30						5:30
6:00						6:00
6:30						6:30
7:00						7:00
7:30						7:30
8:30						8:30

APPENDIX G
WRITING STANDARD OPERATING PROCEDURES

There are several excellent guides to developing standard operating procedures (SOPs). Here are a set of resources that you can look through to find a format that suits your team:

The Brewers Association has a template available at https://www.brewersassociation.org/educational -publications/standard-operating-procedures -guidance-for-brewers/

Quality Management: Essential Planning for Breweries by Mary Pellettieri
"Appendix F: Standard Operating Procedures (SOP) Example"

Quality Labs for Small Brewers: Building a Foundation for Great Beer by Merritt Waldron
"Appendix C: How to Write an SOP"

Seminars on writing SOPs have been presented at both the Craft Brewers Conference® and the MBAA's Master Brewers Conference. Slide decks and seminar recordings are often available by requesting the conference proceedings.

Another option is the following guideline and template. It was developed by Evan Meffert (friend and former colleague of the author) and can be quickly implemented by smaller teams and breweries. All the core components are present: a clear overview of the objectives, safety and quality considerations, procedural steps, a troubleshooting table, and space for document control.

HOW TO STRUCTURE AN SOP

Overview
You want to standardize your processes without sacrificing your ability to be nimble and creative at the operator level. The overview is a snapshot of the procedure, focusing on the broader concepts: why you do this procedure, how you do it, and how it fits into the greater operation of making awesome beer. The overview should be very concise. Someone who knows the task relatively well should be able to read this, get the gist, and perform the task successfully based on their knowledge of the process. Aim for no more than four sentences.

Safety and Important Warnings
Write in very readable terms about the inherent risks of the procedure, e.g., chemical exposure, hearing loss, bodily injury, or electrocution.
- Safe work practice is the #1 priority of everyone
- Unsafe procedures are not tolerated
- Bad communication about potential dangers can lead to unsafe procedures

Quality Impact
Non-standardized work procedures always lead to quality impacts. Consistent beer is a necessary condition for high-quality beer.
- How does following these procedures ensure quality?
- How does failure to follow this procedure detract from quality?

Task Details
Write the steps required in the order they are required. This is the real meat of the SOP and details the work to be done, fleshing out the first page overview.
- Someone who has never seen the equipment before should be able to read this section, comprehend it, and perform the task successfully.
- This section should include an in-depth walkthrough of how the work should be completed, referencing the first page overview when possible and how the working space will look to the operator.

Troubleshooting Table
This table should contain any commonly encountered problems or error codes that may be associated with the procedure and their remedies.

Remarks/Error Codes	Faults	Causes	Remedy

Action/Reaction Plans

This section should contain any action plans and communication guidelines for the operator to follow in the event of an unsuccessful or compromised procedure.

- What actions should be taken?
- Who needs to be notified if something goes wrong?

Revision History

11/12/2022: Added Revision History Subheading

General Notes for the Writer

Aim to simplify the SOP. Minimize page count, while being sure to cover all salient information. Write for the reader, not the writer.

Update the revision history with a new line for the date and what was updated.

APPENDIX H
BASIC PERFORMANCE ASSESSMENT TEMPLATE

This assessment is drawn directly from the Job Description in appendix B. A well-written job description can double as a performance assessment with minimal adjustment.

The rating scale is relatively simple but it communicates the necessary information. Remember that this is a performance assessment, not a disciplinary action. Situations that call for "Needs improvement" indicate that there is a need for coaching. If more is required, there are likely disciplinary issues that need to be resolved.

Note the self-evaluation field: giving employees a chance to evaluate themselves prior to sitting down with their manager provides an opportunity for two-way conversation.

BASIC PERFORMANCE ASSESSMENT — ASSISTANT BREWER

Name: _____ Date: _____

Self-evaluation: Yes   No

Rating	Rating definition
5	Excellent (consistently exceeds standards)
4	Outstanding (frequently exceeds standards)
3	Satisfactory (generally meets standards)
2	Needs improvement (frequently fails to meet standards)
1	Unacceptable (fails to meet standards)

Core Responsibilities

- Communicates and treats fellow coworkers and brewery partners and guests with respect
  - Rating: _____
  - Comments/Notes

- Adheres to a "safety always" mindset and complies with safety policies and programs
  - Rating: _____
  - Comments/Notes

- Approaches every task with quality in mind, paying attention to detail and accuracy
  - Rating: _____
  - Comments/Notes

- Maintains a clean and organized workspace in accordance with food safety regulations
  - Rating: _____
  - Comments/Notes

- Cleans and sanitizes all vessels (brewhouse vessels, fermentors, bright beer tanks, and packaging equipment)
  - Rating: _____
  - Comments/Notes

- Work performance — Rating: _____
  - Brewhouse tasks
    - Comments/Notes

  - Fermentation tasks
    - Comments/Notes

  - Packaging tasks
    - Comments/Notes

  - Sensory evaluation panels
    - Comments/Notes

- Assists with preventive maintenance tasks
  - Rating: _____
  - Comments/Notes

- Ensures that paperwork and associated reporting is done accurately and on time
  - Rating: _____
  - Comments/Notes

- Maintains an inventory of raw materials and brewery supplies, including receiving materials
  - Rating: _____
  - Comments/Notes

- Troubleshooting, technical maintenance, and quality assurance
  - Rating: _____
  - Comments/Notes

- Assists other departments when needed
  - Rating: _____
  - Comments/Notes

Acknowledgments

Employee: _____   Manager: _____

APPENDIX I
EXAMPLE ENGAGEMENT SURVEY QUESTIONS

The following questions are designed to assess workplace culture and employee engagement over time. Individual survey results have some utility, but it is the trends over time that provide usable information about the organizational culture within your brewery. Consistency is the key.

As a rule, the longer the list of questions, the less likely people are to fill out the survey. Not every topic or question needs to be included in the questionnaire. Even three to four questions covering a handful of topics can identify trendlines.

Focus on the areas that you feel best fit your organization's needs. Importantly, these should also be areas that you're willing to work on and invest in to make improvements. Don't ask questions and then avoid taking action on the results.

SURVEY TEMPLATE

The corresponding appendix J shows a formatted listing of these questions (the file can be downloaded from the Brewers Association website's resource hub). You can, of course, take questions from elsewhere and drop them into a spreadsheet format.

The spreadsheet format is also readily mapped onto survey software templates, such as those offered by SurveyMonkey. Software services like this allow surveys to be easily anonymized. Alternatively, small breweries can rely on the low-tech solution of printing the formatted survey and letting employees return them anonymously.

SAMPLE QUESTIONS

General Satisfaction

- My work is challenging, stimulating, and rewarding.
- I am proud to tell people that I work for this organization.
- I am paid fairly for the work I do.

NOTE: If the surveys are genuinely anonymous, the following are options:
- I have applied for another job outside this organization in the past six months.
- If I was offered the same type of job for the same pay at another company, I would decline the offer.

Mission and Values

- I have a good understanding of the mission and the goals of the brewery.
- Leadership provides me with regular information about the brewery's goals.
- I understand how my work directly contributes to the overall success of the organization.
- Doing my job well gives me a sense of personal satisfaction.

Teamwork and Communication

- Teamwork is encouraged and practiced in this organization.
- I receive feedback that helps me improve my performance.
- I have an opportunity to participate in the goal-setting process.
- When I perform well, I receive the praise and recognition I deserve.
- Information and knowledge are shared openly within this organization.

Work-Life Balance

- The environment in this organization supports a balance between work and personal life.
- I am able to satisfy both my professional and personal responsibilities.
- The pace of the work in this organization enables me to do a good job.
- The amount of work I am asked to do is reasonable.
- My job does not cause unreasonable stress in my life.

Respect for Employees

- I am comfortable sharing my opinions at work.
- Leadership makes a genuine effort to attract and develop people with diverse backgrounds.
- People with different ideas are valued in the brewery.
- My ideas and opinions are valued by my coworkers and leaders.
- My manager treats me with respect.
- My coworkers care about me as a person.

Performance and Accountability

- Poor performance is effectively addressed throughout this organization.
- People are held accountable for achieving goals and meeting expectations.
- Job performance is measured consistently across the entire company, without favoritism or bias.
- I have genuine opportunities for professional growth at the brewery.
- Brewery leadership encourages and supports my professional development.

APPENDIX J
ENGAGEMENT
SURVEY TEMPLATE

This template can be used to measure staff engagement. It is developed from the questions in Appendix I. It can easily be customized to fit your needs. The Brewers Association Human Resources Committee has developed an engagement survey tool that can be downloaded from the Resource Hub at BrewersAssociation.org.

General Satisfaction	Strongly Disagree	Disagree	Somewhat Disagree	Somewhat Agree	Agree	Strongly Agree
My work is challenging, stimulating, and rewarding.	○	○	○	○	○	○
I am proud to tell people that I work for this organization.	○	○	○	○	○	○
I am paid fairly for the work I do.	○	○	○	○	○	○

Mission and Values	Strongly Disagree	Disagree	Somewhat Disagree	Somewhat Agree	Agree	Strongly Agree
I have a good understanding of the mission and the goals of the brewery.	○	○	○	○	○	○
Leadership provides me with regular information about the brewery's goals.	○	○	○	○	○	○
I understand how my work directly contributes to the overall success of the organization.	○	○	○	○	○	○
Doing my job well gives me a sense of personal satisfaction.	○	○	○	○	○	○

Teamwork and Communication	Strongly Disagree	Disagree	Somewhat Disagree	Somewhat Agree	Agree	Strongly Agree
Teamwork is encouraged and practiced in this organization.	○	○	○	○	○	○
I receive feedback that helps me improve my performance.	○	○	○	○	○	○
I have an opportunity to participate in the goal-setting process.	○	○	○	○	○	○
When I perform well, I receive the praise and recognition I deserve.	○	○	○	○	○	○
Information and knowledge are shared openly within this organization.	○	○	○	○	○	○

Work-Life Balance	Strongly Disagree	Disagree	Somewhat Disagree	Somewhat Agree	Agree	Strongly Agree
The environment in this organization supports a balance between work and personal life.	○	○	○	○	○	○
I am able to satisfy both my professional and personal responsibilities.	○	○	○	○	○	○
The pace of the work in this organization enables me to do a good job.	○	○	○	○	○	○
The amount of work I am asked to do is reasonable.	○	○	○	○	○	○
My job does not cause unreasonable stress in my life.	○	○	○	○	○	○

Respect for Employees	Strongly Disagree	Disagree	Somewhat Disagree	Somewhat Agree	Agree	Strongly Agree
I am comfortable sharing my opinions at work.	○	○	○	○	○	○
Leadership makes a genuine effort to attract and develop people with diverse backgrounds.	○	○	○	○	○	○
People with different ideas are valued in the brewery.	○	○	○	○	○	○
My ideas and opinions are valued by my coworkers and leaders.	○	○	○	○	○	○
My manager treats me with respect.	○	○	○	○	○	○
My coworkers care about me as a person.	○	○	○	○	○	○

Performance and Accountability	Strongly Disagree	Disagree	Somewhat Disagree	Somewhat Agree	Agree	Strongly Agree
Poor performance is effectively addressed throughout this organization.	○	○	○	○	○	○
People are held accountable for achieving goals and meeting expectations.	○	○	○	○	○	○
Job performance is measured consistently across the entire company, without favoritism or bias.	○	○	○	○	○	○
I have genuine opportunities for professional growth at the brewery.	○	○	○	○	○	○
Brewery leadership encourages and supports my professional development.	○	○	○	○	○	○

BIBLIOGRAPHY

Barzun, Matthew. 2021. *The Power of Giving Away Power: How the Best Leaders Learn to Let Go*. New York: Optimism Press.

Berkley, Robyn A., and David M. Kaplan. 2020. *Strategic Training and Development*. Thousand Oaks, CA: SAGE Publications Inc.

Dimock, Michael. 2019. "Defining generations: Where Millennials end and Generation Z begins." Pew Research Center. Published January 17, 2019. https://www.pewresearch.org/fact-tank/2019/01/17 /where-millennials-end-and-generation-z-begins/.

Gawande, Atul. 2009. *The Checklist Manifesto: How to Get Things Right*. New York: Metropolitan Books.

Haslam, Holly. 2022. *Recognizing Substance Use Disorder in the Craft Beer Industry*. Boulder, CO: Brewers Association. https://www.brewersassociation.org/educational-publications/recognizing-substance -use-disorder-in-the-craft-beer-industry/.

Heath, Chip, and Dan Heath. 2007. *Made to Stick: Why Some Ideas Survive and Others Die*. New York: Random House.

Holle, Stephen R., Ray Klimovitz, Lars Larson, Karl Ockert, and Steve Presley, eds. 2012. *Beer Steward Handbook: A Practical Guide to Understanding Beer*. 2nd ed. St. Paul, MN: Master Brewers Association of the Americas.

Jackson-Beckham, J. 2022. "Hiring Bias: It's More Than Just Cultural Stereotypes." *New Brewer*, July/August 2022. http://onlinedigitalpublishing.com/publication/?i=753635&p=80&view=issueViewer.

Ken Blanchard Companies. 2020. "Managing Coaching for Results and ROI." White paper, Ken Blanchard Companies, Escondido, CA. https://resources.kenblanchard.com/whitepapers/managing-coaching -for-results-and-roi.

Klimovitz, Ray. 2012. "Whirlpool." In *Oxford Companion to Beer*, edited by Garrett Oliver. Oxford University Press.

Masnick, George. 2017. "Defining the generations redux." Housing Perspectives [blog]. Joint Center for Housing Studies of Harvard University. Published February 16, 2017. https://www.jchs.harvard.edu/blog /defining-the-generations-redux.

McCord, Patty. 2017. *Powerful: Building a Culture of Freedom and Responsibility*. Silicon Guild.

Mosher, Randy. 2009. *Tasting Beer: An Insider's Guide to the World's Greatest Drink*. North Adams, MA: Storey Publishing.

Oliver, Garrett, ed. 2012. *Oxford Companion to Beer*. Oxford University Press.

Page, Scott E. 2007. *The Difference: How the Power of Diversity Creates Better Groups, Firms, Schools, and Societies*. Princeton, NJ: Princeton University Press.

———. 2017. *The Diversity Bonus: How Great Teams Pay Off in the Knowledge Economy*. Princeton, NJ: Princeton University Press.

Pan, Steven C. 2015. "The Interleaving Effect: Mixing It Up Boosts Learning." *Scientific American*, August 4, 2015. https://www.scientificamerican.com/article/the-interleaving-effect-mixing-it-up-boosts-learning/.

Pellettieri, Mary. 2015. *Quality Management: Essential Planning for Breweries*. Boulder, CO: Brewers Publications.

Pellettieri, Mary, and Gary Nicholas. 2020. *Food Safety Planning for Craft Brewers: Brewing a Food Safe Beer; Best Practice and Regulatory Compliance with the Food Safety Modernization Act*. Boulder, CO: Brewers Association.

Quality Subcommittee. 2020. *Standard Operating Procedures Guidance for Brewers*. Boulder, CO: Brewers Association. https://www.brewersassociation.org/educational-publications/standard-operating-procedures-guidance-for-brewers/.

Rath, Tom, and Barry Conchie. 2008. *Strengths Based Leadership: Great Leaders, Teams, and Why People Follow*. New York: Gallup Press.

Sinek, Simon. 2014. *Leaders Eat Last: Why Some Teams Pull Together and Others Don't*. New York: Portfolio/Penguin.

Waldron, Merritt. 2020. *Quality Labs for Small Brewers: Building a Foundation for Great Beer*. Boulder, CO: Brewers Publications.

INDEX

platforms, 30, 59, 65; application, 14, 15; sales, 60; software, 88

policy, 73, 81; people as, 90; previewing, 79; reviewing, 107, 108

pool model, 109

positive reinforcement, 93

postings, 10–14, 15, 108; examples of, 113–18; writing, 11–14

pre-shift meetings, 81; agenda for, 59 (fig.); described, 58–59

Preventive Control Qualified Individual (PCQI), 52

priorities, 11, 16, 122; accountability and, 3; focusing on, 90; managing, 87; organizational, 2, 3; teams and, 1

problem-solving, 13, 20, 42, 44, 66, 103, 105

procedures, 94; complaint, 95; defining, 93

process, 33; breaking down, 40; honesty about, 13; simplifying, 92

process and instrumentation diagrams (P&IDs), 40

product mixes, 80

production, 7, 32, 34, 50, 59, 133; evaluating, 62; reduced, 98

production leadership: communication skills for, 64; evaluation categories for, 62 (table)

production operator, evaluation categories for, 62 (table)

production training checklist, sample, 131–40

professional development, 3, 10, 24, 33, 47, 56, 85, 111; addressing, 60; building, 21; burnout and, 99; innovation through, 105; management skills and, 50; opportunities for, 51, 106; proficiency, 43; developing, 42 (fig.); establishing, 41–42

program reviews, 107; questions for, 108

programmable logic controller (PLC), 53

qualifications, 115; desired, 124; trap, 12

quality, 9, 37, 48, 59, 77, 81, 101; awareness of, 73; as culture, 93; evaluating, 62; implications for, 94; training and, 44

quality assurance, 66, 103

quality assurance and quality control (QA/QC), 2

Quality Labs for Small Brewers, 107

Quality Management, 107

questions: closed-loop, 16; follow-up, 16; interview, 14–17; open-loop, 17; performance-related, 17

race, 55, 97

reaction plans, 37–38, 66, 72

READ-DO checklists, 38

recordkeeping, 44

recruiting, 7, 13, 23, 111

regulatory compliance, 29, 30–31

rejections, handling, 24–25

resilience, 8, 22, 111; culture and, 3–4

Resource Hub, 96

resources, 51–53, 86, 107, 109; access to, 98; developing/promoting, 99; financial, 106; lack of, 28; managing, 1–2; providing, 105. *See also* human resources

respect, 72, 73

responsibilities, 12, 13, 51, 114, 116; core, 123; designating, 99

responsiveness, 94–95

résumés, 10, 20, 21, 22, 23; reviewing, 14–17, 24

retention rates, 4, 21, 39, 42, 44, 63

return on investment (ROI), 2

reviewing, 17, 63, 64

Rhodes, Elle, 3, 20

role models, negative, 71

run phase, 41–42

safety, 28, 30, 33, 37, 48, 59, 72, 77, 101, 133; audits, 107; awareness, of, 73; evaluating, 62; food, 31, 35; implications for, 94; operator, 35; psychological, 99; training and, 44

safety expectations, scoring, 64 (table)

safety issues, 48, 81; reporting, 30–31

sales, 8–9, 32, 38, 47, 89; task/metric of, 18

SAMPLE, described, 36

sanitation programs, 9, 28, 31, 38, 39, 93

SanTan Brewery, 105

scheduling, 59, 77, 80, 81; simplifying, 48

selection, 108; evaluation and, 17–25

self-awareness, 98, 109

self-ratings, 63–64, 64–65

sense of purpose, 87–88, 111

sensor packages, 12

sensory evaluation, 2, 49

separations, handling, 67

Serendipity Brewing, 9

sexual assaults and harassment (SAH), reality of, 95

shift rotations, 103; example of, 104 (fig.)

Siebel Institute of Technology, 27, 52

Sierra Nevada, collaboration at, 104

skills, 14, 15, 17, 18, 29, 77, 81, 94, 96, 102, 107, 111, 116; advanced, 47, 51–53; assessing, 21, 34, 42–43; communication, 61, 64; computer, 53; core, 22; critical, 47; crossover, 48; desired, 12; developing, 10, 48, 57, 103; focus on, 19–20; interpersonal,